Books and plays by DORE SCHARY

CASE HISTORY OF A MOVIE

SUNRISE AT CAMPOBELLO

THE HIGHEST TREE

THE DEVIL'S ADVOCATE
  (dramatization of book by Morris L. West)

FOR SPECIAL OCCASIONS

For Special Occasions

FOR
SPECIAL
OCCASIONS

Dore Schary

Random House

New York

"Who's the Rabbi?" has appeared in slightly different form in the winter 1961 issue of *American Judaism*.

Thanks are due the following for permission to quote:

ALL ABOARD FOR BLANKET BAY, p. 196: By special permission of Harry Von Tilzer Music Publishing Company; copyrighted 1910.

AMERICA I LOVE YOU, p. 13: Copyright 1915 Mills Music, Inc.; copyright renewed 1942. Used by permission of the copyright owners, Mills Music, Inc. and Mr. Edgar Leslie.

DEAR OLD GIRL, p. 5: Courtesy Shawnee Press, Inc., Delaware Water Gap, Pa., for the world outside of the U.S.A.

FOR YOUR BOY AND MY BOY, pp. 58 and 59: Copyright 1918 by Remick Music Corporation. Reprinted by permission.

KEEP YOUR HEAD DOWN "FRITZIE BOY," p. 59: Words and music by Lieut. Gitz Rice. © Copyright 1918/copyright renewal 1946 Leo Feist, Inc., New York, N.Y. Used by permission.

LONG BOY, p. 59: Copyright MCMXVII by Shapiro, Bernstein & Co. Inc.; copyright renewed MCMXLIV and assigned to Shapiro, Bernstein & Co. Inc., 666 Fifth Avenue, New York 19, New York. Used by permission of the publisher.

SECOND PRINTING

Library of Congress Catalog Card Number: 62–12735

MANUFACTURED IN THE UNITED STATES OF AMERICA
BY AMERICAN BOOK–STRATFORD PRESS, INC., NEW YORK
Design by Tere LoPrete

This book is dedicated to my grandchildren with a hope and a prayer.

The hope is that when they are old enough to read and understand, the stories will tell them something of value about a world they never knew.

The prayer is that the world in which they will be living will be a fruitful and peaceful one for them and all their contemporaries.

Author's Note

Recently I visited Newark, and though it was no surprise to find that you can't go home any more, the changes seemed unusually severe. One section of town of which I write in this book has been leveled to make way for a needed housing development. The homes on Thirteenth Avenue, where I lived, have been bulldozed and the earth flattened for parking lots. The shift of population and the changing economy have altered the face of the city. The splendiferous old Prudential Insurance Company building, with its gray granite gargoyles, has been replaced by a spanking new structure in the modern ice-tray style of architecture.

But enough landmarks were there to re-establish old memories and bring some of these stories back to life. Though I've changed some names for obvious reasons, the stories are true, and I've determined to write them before fancy catches up with fact.

Contents

For Special Occasions

1

"It Gives Me Great Pleasure"

As a young master of ceremonies I often introduced guest artists and members of my family who performed at the affairs held at our boarding houses, hotels and catering places. In those days (and, alas, sometimes in these days) the usual introduction took the form of the title of this first chapter. Since I am writing about those days, it gives me great pleasure at this time to present the members of my family: my father, Herman Hugo Schary, my mother, Belle Schary, my sisters, Lillian and Frances, my brother, Sam, my maternal grandparents, Baruch and Shaina Drachler, and various uncles, aunts and cousins.

These stories are about our family during the World War I period, and about the place where we lived and worked, a kosher catering establishment called Schary Manor in Newark, New Jersey.

My father was born in Riga in 1873. His father was a ladies' and gentlemen's custom tailor. My paternal grandfather was a small, meticulous man, who walked with a quick, brisk step; his Vandyke beard and his mustache, both sharply pointed, were always well barbered. He spoke German and remained a martinet until his lonely death at the age of eighty-three. We always called him Grosspapa. He spawned a large family by two wives, who were sisters, but he never succeeded in being close to any of his children.

After a bitter quarrel with Grosspapa my father left home in Riga when he was fourteen years old. He traveled to England, sold matches on street corners, went into the cigar business, and returned to Riga when he was eighteen, sporting a fur-lined overcoat, beautifully tailored custom clothes, a silver-headed cane and a top hat. Grosspapa greeted the triumphal return of the prodigal by slapping him across the cheek, a gesture he had delayed when my father had left home four years before.

Then my father set out for America—the long way. He went to Moscow, then by rail to Vladivostok, then to Japan, and landed in San Francisco in 1892. His next stop was Brooklyn, where he met my mother. They fell in love and were married in 1895, when she was twenty and he was twenty-two.

In his early days my pa was a tall, lean man. He wore a thin mustache for a few years, then got rid of it. A long time later he grew a thick black one, but by then he was heavier and it made him look like Pancho Villa. He shaved it off after enduring for a couple of years the bad jokes that came with it.

In 1914 Pa weighed two hundred and twenty-two pounds. Whenever he was asked his weight he would say, "I am two-two-two too much." He had a shock of dark hair which didn't get gray until he was in his fifties, and his hands and arms were powerful and destructive aids to a heroic temper. Among his talents was a gift for story telling. He sang quite well, and he knew bits of various operas and the folk songs of many nations. Often he would recount his early adventures and sing these songs to us; some of them I've sung to my children and now to my grandchildren. Pa also sang such popular American songs as "All Aboard for Blanket Bay," "Dear Old Girl (The robin sings above you)," "Isle d'Amour" and "The Turkey Trot." Though he appeared soft and somewhat flabby, he could lift a good-sized cash register—and did so once on a bet that earned him a hundred dollars when he needed it badly. It also earned him a hernia which he didn't have repaired until he was seventy.

Pa's talents and ambitions were multiple and versatile. He was an excellent and imaginative window dresser, and for a time he decorated bars with colored soaps for holiday celebrations. (He also decorated public buildings on national holidays. But he had to give this up when he fell off a scaffold and broke his leg while draping bunting at the Newark Courthouse on the occasion of President McKinley's assassination.)

Pa's huge hands could sew delicate golden designs on red velvet; he could also break an oar with them. His interest in furnishings led him to collect fancy bric-a-brac and Victorian statuary and porcelain. Dreams of conquest pursued him all his life. When he was in the catering and hotel business he had visions of owning a chain of catering places and hotels all over the East

Coast. Years later, when he fell upon hard times, he owned a miniature golf course, and dreamed of owning thousands of them spread from New York to California. They were to be called the Schary Hole-in-One Golf Association.

Like his father, Pa preferred German to Yiddish, but he could also speak Polish, some Russian, a dash of Swedish (where he learned the latter none of us ever knew) and a careful and rather florid English with occasional and unique malapropisms and mispronunciations.

Papa believed in full and generous living. His wardrobe was huge and chosen with great taste. Though he didn't drink and smoked few cigars, he was an avid and reckless pinochle player and a ravenous eater. He was courteous and particularly gallant to women, who were as attracted to him as he to them. On those holidays or for family celebrations when he took us to New York, he arranged for orchestra seats in the theatre and the best table at Delmonico's or Lorber's, ordered the finest food and champagne and tipped the waiters lavishly.

Pa's favorite dream was to own a tract of some twenty or thirty heavily wooded acres. Each one of the children would have a separate home for his family, but the center of this feudal arrangement would be the big baronial house where Mother and he would live. In it would be a bowling alley, poolroom, music room and various entertainments, including of course lots of statues and vases and bric-a-brac.

Except when he went into one of his rages, Pa's behavior was gentlemanly. As he struggled to control his mounting wrath he would become even more polite, and so when we heard him address someone with "Excuse me, sir, pardon me, but may I ask you, sir, to be kind enough to leave the premises—," we knew that he was about to explode.

My mother was born in Bialystok, Russia, in 1875. At one time her father, Baruch Drachler, was a musician and soldier in the Czar's army. When he was drafted into service he obtained a religious divorce from my grandmother, Shaina. This was a common practice among Jewish draftees because of a Jewish law which forbids a widow to remarry when, in the absence of a body, there is no positive proof of her husband's death. Since service in the army offered that distinct possibility, Jewish warriors obtained a *geht*, a religious divorce, which would free their women to remarry in the event they were reported missing in action. When my *zaida* (grandfather) went into the service of Czar Alexander III, my mother was ten years old and her sister, Bessie, three years old. When Zaida returned safely after three years' service and no war, my mother and her sister were present at the second wedding of their parents.

The Drachlers fled the continued oppression and pogroms in Russia and came to America via Hamburg and Ellis Island in 1891. They arrived in New York on February 12, my mother's sixteenth birthday. Most of their belongings were stolen by porters, who used to prey on the flood of unsuspecting "greenhorns" immigrating at that time. The family settled in Brooklyn, where Zaida got employment as a hat maker and my mother went to work in a shirt factory.

Zaida was a straight, tall man with a full and well-trimmed gray beard. He always wore a *yarmalke*—not one of those dainty little skull caps sitting on the back of his head, but a tall, crowned one that sat squarely and completely on his head. He was learned in the Talmud and spoke half a dozen languages.

There was another member of the family, Mother's brother, Jacob—Jack—who was two years old when they arrived in the United States. Jack grew up to look like my grandfather, but he was shorter, and he lacked my grandfather's character and will.

Both my mother and my Aunt Bessie were beautiful women—as was their mother, whom they both resembled—and all three of them labored hard in their homes and at their work. Mother was a magnificent cook with "golden hands." She had the remarkable ability to prepare chicken soup for eight hundred people, and when the eight hundred were served, the soup kettles would contain only enough soup to take care of the few extra who might show up unexpectedly. She could never give a recipe; if you wanted to learn you had to watch her. Her seasoning of food was part of the magic, and if you asked her, "How much salt or sugar?" she'd say, "You'll know. You can feel it."

Mother was patient and polite to everyone. She spoke and read Yiddish, Polish, Russian, Hungarian, German and English. She was a marvelous mimic and shrewder about people than my father, and also far more tolerant. She seldom lost her temper and never struck any of us, but she was not permissive and demanded that we do those tasks that we were assigned. She was straight and tall and carried herself with grace and style. Her eyes were china blue, her complexion radiant, and her hands remained soft after forty years of hard kitchen work. During her years of work in Schary Manor, Mother displayed magical gifts of recuperation from fatigue. When she had finished her labors in the kitchen and knew that everyone was taken care of, she would go to her room and reappear an hour later looking like the Queen of the Ball. The guests would make her the center of attention and listen to her stories and wonder how she could look so well rested.

Both my parents were blessed with a large capacity for work and inexhaustible energy. After they were married in Brooklyn they settled down to running a small restaurant and delicatessen, which my father had decorated with his own hands and his own ideas. My brother Sam was born in Brooklyn a year after the marriage. Two years later another son, Max, was born; he died of brain fever eighteen months later.

The restaurant in Brooklyn failed at about the time that Zaida had made contact with some of his friends from Russia who had settled in Newark. The family decided to move there and join the *shtetel*, or Jewish community, which was orthodox and familiar. They moved near the heart of the colony, which was located on Prince Street. Nearby was the orthodox Anshe Russia synagogue, presided over by Rabbi Brodsky.

That section of Newark was a thriving Jewish community in those years. A walk through Prince Street would be rewarded by the smell of freshly baked rye bread, matjes herring, spicy corned beef, newly ground coffee, sawdust, kosher slaughtered chicken and all kinds of scale fish, the sharp smell of radishes, cucumbers and other vegetables on pushcarts. It was a hustling, cackling area, and the competition between merchants was as brisk and aggressive as the bargaining between merchant and customer.

On Mulberry Street my parents opened another restaurant, but nothing of importance happened during this time except the births of my sisters, Frances and Lillian, two years apart.

The Scharys kept moving and working. Pa was now dressing store windows and bars; Mother was selling greeting cards, a door-to-door business in those days. They owned a carriage and a horse named Jimmy, which was used to convey Mother from Newark to Elizabeth or Passaic or Harrison.

I was born on Charlton Street in 1905. My mother told me that when I was born I was greeted by a neighbor who had helped Dr. Danzis with the delivery. She took one look at me and murmured, *"Oi vey, finster is mir,"* which is best rendered in English, "Dear me, what a misfortune." Apparently I was a homely child.

As fortunes improved, the family moved to Court Street; then, as employment dwindled, to Thirteenth Avenue. Pa had embarked on a new career selling real estate. When, much to his surprise, he made a particularly handsome commission, we moved to a larger apartment in a four-family house, also on Thirteenth Avenue. Here we finally had our own bathroom and multicolored ceiling fixtures that combined gas mantles and electric lights. Now, because of Pa's increased income, Mother was able to concentrate more on the family. Prosperity brought us an upright piano, a four-piece living-room suite made of mahogany and green velours, and a stunning variety of vases and bronze statues of properly draped ladies and gentlemen of ample anatomy. One of the ladies had a clock in her stomach. It was difficult to know whether Mother approved or disapproved of these purchases; she'd merely say, "Oh, Hugo."

Then the real estate business had one of its periodic recessions. On request, Mother began to make extra food for neighbors who wanted her gefilte fish for Friday night or her borscht for warm summer suppers or her roast, stuffed chicken for special occasions.

A neighbor of ours, Louis Lasser, who owned a men's clothing store, had a daughter named Susan who was to be married. The Lassers, who lived in the house directly opposite our apartment, asked Mother if she would provide the food for the wedding—if she would cater the affair. Mother agreed, and that is how the idea of Schary Manor was born. Father decorated the Lasser apartment with hand-picked black-eyed Susans (in honor of the bride), and Mother, aided in this first effort by my grandmother, turned out her best food.

After this satisfactory debut, there were additional demands from friends in the neighborhood to whom lavish weddings were a status symbol in 1913. By early 1914 Father had found a house on High Street that was large enough for a catering establishment and within his means.

At that time the move from Thirteenth Avenue to High Street might be compared roughly to moving from Hester Street to Park Avenue in New York. We were leaving the cobblestones for the pavement.

High Street was the best residential street in Newark and was dominated by large and lovely early nineteenth-century homes. The street was well populated with reputable doctors and respected lawyers. Gottfried Kreuger, the famous brewery baron, lived in an expensive red sandstone castle just across the street; close by lived the Wosnitzers, the Frelingheusens, the Hollanders, who were fur merchants, and a host of rich and snobbish German Jews, who had built a beautiful temple some blocks from us. Here, too, was the best music studio in Newark, owned by Mandel and Rosalie Svet, teachers of piano, violin and harmony. Respectability required that one's children learn to play violin or piano, and music lessons were a must along with classes at *cheder* (Hebrew school).

With the purchase of Schary Manor my father was in his element, and he went to work with decorating schemes that included collages, statues on pedestals and gilded cherubs suspended over the area where the wedding canopy, the *chupah*, would be placed. Various wallpaper designs adorned the walls, as well as painted murals and panels with inset mirrors. There was a Green Room, a Blue Room, a Gold Room and an Oak Room.

Schary Manor was a roaring, storming success from the very beginning. Jewish families flocked to the Scharys at 584 High Street for their sons' bar mitzvahs, their weddings, their twenty-fifth anniversaries, their birthdays and their charity banquets.

In a few months Zaida and my grandmother (*bubeh*) came to live with us. Zaida's assignment was to make certain that everything was strictly kosher, and Bubeh was to help out in the kitchen. In this house my parents assembled their staff, which was to remain with them for years. This included our Number-One chef, Mr. Fleischer (known to everyone only as Fleischer—if he had a first name, none of us ever learned it); Sidney Rapp, an ex-prizefighter and a waiter, who became our chief kitchen assistant and handyman; Frank Monahan, the head waiter; and Rosie Carter, a Negro of Amazonian proportions, who captained a staff of colored girls who cared for the silver and china, laundered the napkins and tablecloths, and kept the pantries clean.

Rosie was so conscientious that in a short time she knew more about what was kosher than most of us.

Within two years the business could not be accommodated at 584, so Father purchased the mansion of Senator Smith, the New Jersey political boss, at 604 High Street. This imposing and beautifully designed house was four stories tall and was made of brownstone and light brown brick. Again Father burgeoned with ideas. He built a large banquet room at the back of the house, which had been repainted, redecorated and redesigned. A handsome sign, proudly declaring "Schary Manor, Catering for Special Occasions," was installed in front.

When we moved into the house we were also moving into an era of our lives that was to last from 1916 to 1924. It was the time when Newark was growing into a large city; when the Jewish community was straining out of its cramped self-imposed ghetto and groping its way into American life; when America was growing fat, sassy and strong; when we sang "America, I Love You (And there's a hundred million others like me)." It was the time when "Hatikvah," now the national anthem of the State of Israel, was only "A Hope," as the song title stated. It was the time when the first generation of Jews, along with their immigrant parents and grandparents, were testing the promise of this new land of freedom and decided it would be enduring.

This book is about that time, those people and that place in Newark,

SCHARY MANOR

CATERING

FOR SPECIAL OCCASIONS

2

The Haunted House

When we lived on Thirteenth Avenue, before moving to High Street, I was eight years old. With some of my more adventuresome friends, like Harold Lasser, Jack Gold and Fred Leamy, I used to walk from our poor neighborhood to visit the rich folks on High Street.

We would march up Springfield Avenue, past St. Benedict's Academy, which was a Catholic parochial high school. We were always prepared for a brawl, but Fred Leamy, who was Irish and a Catholic, had a pug nose and red hair, and he provided safe escort for us.

Beyond St. Benedict's was the Newark Academy, a private school on the corner of High and William streets. Because it was private and was attended by sons of rich men, we assumed that the boys at the school were all sissies. To us, "sissies" was a term used for all inept street fighters, cowards, crybabies and sons of rich people. Often we would stop at the fence surrounding the Academy and watch the polite young men as they practiced tumbling or baseball. Regulated sports were beneath us; we had grown up in a neighborhood where One O' Cat, Red Rover, Pinch and Ouch, Run Chief Run, and Johnny on the Pony were played for keeps. A protest over rules usually ended the game and started a free-for-all. It wasn't that we were bad losers; it was just that everybody wanted to win. So whenever we saw games played properly, as we always did at the Academy, we scoffed and mocked the players.

The boys usually ignored us, which only made us more furious and more vocal. One day a handsome young man came to the fence and told us to go away. Fred Leamy, our best fighter and the tallest member of our group, invited him out to the pavement to settle the question of whether we should depart or not. Much to our surprise, the young man vaulted the four-foot fence and took a fighting stance. We stepped back as Fred circled his well-dressed opponent. Some of the other Academy scholars gathered near the fence, calling words of encouragement to their gladiator. When we heard his name was Marion, we doubled up with laughter.

Marion paid no attention to this added indignity. He stepped toward the circling Fred and belted him on the jaw; when Fred drew back, Marion hit him in the stomach. Fred keeled over, gasping for breath. Marion looked us over and waited for one of us to step forward to pick up the gauntlet. We were no fools; obviously Marion was a professional boxer who was posing as a student. When we wordlessly declined his challenge, he vaulted back over the fence to the sound of cheers from his colleagues. We helped Freddie to his feet, and thereafter passed the Academy on the opposite side of the street.

When we walked up High Street and looked at the beautifully kept lawns and hedges, there always seemed to be a smell of newly cut grass in the air. Though High Street residents were well ahead of the rest of the town in the acquisition of automobiles, there were also lovely carriages and bay horses parading down the avenue. The girls and boys playing in the streets and on the lawns all had spanking new bicycles, and their clothes were pretty and seemed to fit them better than did ours.

We would rubberneck until a butler or chauffeur would order us away. We always sensed that we were in enemy territory and felt that if we didn't behave we might be apprehended and kept in captivity by the patricians.

At that time there was only one empty house in the block between Mercer and Court streets. This was an old gabled three-story dwelling that had been abandoned years before. Once when we asked a gardener about the house, he told us that someone had died in it by taking poison, and soon after everybody had left because the ghost of the dead person roamed around the place at night clanking chains.

Even at the age of eight I had the mind of an inquiring reporter; I wanted to know why the ghost clanked chains. "All ghosts have chains," I was told disdainfully. Harold Lasser said that of course he knew that.

Jack Gold learned that it was a woman who had taken the poison; the gardener added that she was a rather fearsome-looking woman who wore a large rat. This was the first time I had heard the word "rat" used to describe false hair; since I knew only its rodent meaning, the image of the ghostly lady wearing a real pet rat on her head never left me.

After we heard the story we used to prowl around the outside of the house. We would go into the back yard and peer into the stables, the doors of which had sagged into a permanent opening that enabled us to see in without entering; after all, the ghost might slam the doors behind us.

After a while we were emboldened to look through the back windows of the house. One day Harold Lasser picked up a rock and sailed it through a pane of unbroken glass. We ran back a respectable distance, in fear that the ghost might come to the window and hurl the rock back at us.

After that act of bravery on Harold's part, which had apparently intimidated the ghost, we were more hardy—though we proceeded cautiously. We threw more rocks through the windows, we rattled the bolted rear door, and we looked into the dim and dusty rooms on the first floor. There was not a sign of a ghost.

The conquest of the haunted house became the talk of our group on Thirteenth Avenue, and on our later expeditions we were joined by other friends, including Izzy Schechner and "Dutch" Voorhees. We pretended that we were being generous in letting them in on the sport, but of course we were delighted that now there were more of us to protect each other.

One day Dutch decided we ought to try the front door to see if it was open. We would all go in and explore the interior. We all agreed to this, but the debate centered on who would go first. Since it was Dutch's idea, he finally volunteered. We all supported him by standing well behind him with rocks and sticks. When Dutch tried the door, there was a click as the old door-knob released the lock; then the door opened with a hideous and piercing creaking and squealing. We all backed away in terror. But it was a sunny day and the chance of a ghost with a rat on her head coming to chase six of us seemed unlikely, so we slowly returned.

The sun glancing into the house gave us a view of the darkened hall and the steps leading up to the next floor. Forming a solid wall of quivering courage, we moved to the doorway. There was not a sign of a ghost, nor a sound of clanking chains. Cautiously we nudged each other into the hall. With admirable foresight Jack Gold announced that he would hold the door, so that it couldn't close suddenly. We looked into the side rooms; there was a musty smell of damp and what seemed to be an odor of bath powder. On the floors there were all sorts of stains.

Dutch screwed up his courage to tread on the first step of the flight leading upstairs. Suddenly he yelled, "Hey, you ghost!" We stood riveted, our eyes on the door being held securely open by Jack. But this didn't exorcise the ghost either, so Harold had another idea. He had found some tin cans in the front hall, left, I suppose, by itinerants who had used the place for shelter. (What had happened to them, we didn't dare guess.) In a sudden and explosive charge of bravery, Harold began heaving the cans up the steps to the second floor. The clatter was deafening, and as one of the cans began to roll down the steps in measured cadence, we all knew that the ghost was on her way down. We ran like hell.

Outside, we turned and looked back. And, unbelievably, the front door slowly closed. Dutch, who knew about many things, said that it was because of the draft created by our departure or by the wind blowing through the open windows. But we all knew Dutch was whistling in the dark; that door had closed because *she* closed it.

We hiked back to Thirteenth Avenue and spoke of our adventure to some of the older fellows, who scoffed at us. During supper that night I asked my father if he knew anything about ghosts. Papa said he knew all about them; "Why?" he asked.

I wanted to know if ghosts ever chased anyone outside of the places they haunted. Papa said that was ridiculous; ghosts always stayed where they were, but sometimes by telepathy they could make people come to them. He told us a story of a man who had been cheated by his best friend. After he had died of grief and shock he had been buried in the local cemetery. But one night his false friend had felt impelled to walk through the cemetery, and the next morning he had been found lying dead on the grave of the man he had betrayed. Papa said the ghost had reached up through the ground and grabbed him.

Frances, my older sister, suggested reasonably that perhaps the man's long coat had caught on something and that he had died of fright. Under the circumstances I dismissed Frances' explanation. Here was a clear case of a ghost getting even with an enemy; and that old lady ghost had, I knew, spotted me as her enemy. All of us—Harold, Jack, Izzy, Dutch, Fred and I—were doomed. It was only a matter of the order in which she would choose to will each of us back to her. My friends and I didn't approach that old house any more. We walked past it on the other side of the street, and soon I began to forget the curse that had been laid on us.

Then Harold's sister, Susan, was married. Mother catered the supper and it was so successful that my parents decided to open a catering establishment. I was vaguely aware of their decision, but I didn't know what it meant until one night almost a year later when Mother told us that we were moving to High Street. Father had found a house that was going to be called Schary Manor; it was big and had a back yard and Zaida and Bubeh were coming to live with us.

Our new address was 584 High Street, and of course it was the haunted house. I realized that my time had come, and in sudden panic I told my family the entire tale: I was to be Number One on the lady-ghost's list.

For reasons beyond me at the time, my family paid no attention to my alarms. Pa told me that his story about the two friends was a piece of scary fiction, and my sisters and my brother Sam laughed. Mother said there were no such things as ghosts—and if there were they weren't kosher and would leave the house as soon as we settled into it. But this was one of the few times I did not find my mother's calm reassuring.

When moving day came, my friends bade me farewell; their lurid jokes on the subject weren't funny to me at all. But when we moved in, my fears dwindled. Pa had had the house painted a light cream color, and the rooms inside were cheerful and light. The upstairs bedroom, which I shared with Sam, was airy and streaming with sunshine. I decided that I had been victimized by a gory fable.

For the first few days and nights I kept sniffing about for a scent of the bath powder that I had noticed on that one fearful day when we had broken into the house, but the new paint and varnish had driven it out. So I relaxed, until the night of the first storm that hit after we had moved in. My brother had not yet come home and I was just going to sleep when I heard the low crack of thunder. Then the clouds blacked out the moon, the thunder rolled closer, booming and rattling the windows, and the lightning flashed, creating weird shadows that jumped about the room. I switched on the electric light and breathed a sigh of relief, which was quickly followed by terror as the lights went out. I huddled in my bed and stared out the window. Through the storm I could see lights in nearby houses. Now I knew the worst: the ghost was preparing for her assault on me by turning out our lights. The house moaned with the spatter of heavy rain. I heard a door creak open somewhere on the upper floor, and as my heart thumped with fear, I heard a groan and soft footfalls in the hall. I was too scared to scream, and in the pitch darkness I could see nothing.

Then came a tap on the door and a sad voice hoarsely called my name. I was no fool; I didn't answer. But "she" was not to be stopped, and I heard my door being opened. There was a flash of lightning and in that second of light I saw the robed figure of Joe Gans, one of our boarders. Or was it?

I called out loudly, "Mr. Gans?"

"Yes," he said. "I have a terrible toothache. Can you get me a hot water bottle?"

It was the pleasantest request ever made of me. Happily I ran out of the room into the dark hall; though the entire house was black, except for small pools of light spread by the candles Mother had lighted downstairs, I didn't mind a bit. I raced down the steps and my family seemed as glad to see me as I was to see them. Mother and Lil got the hot water bottle for Mr. Gans along with some camphorated oil, which they advised him to rub on his gums, and he went back to bed.

I stayed downstairs with the family. We sat in Mother's and Father's room and Pa sang songs to us and Zaida told us stories of the old country. The rushing noise of water in the gutters diminished to the soft pitter-patter of a fading rainstorm, and the moonlight appeared again through the bay window. Miraculously the electric power was restored.

By now Sam had come home, and we went upstairs to bed. When I confessed to him how scared I had been, he told me I was being stupid; there were no such things as ghosts. He told me to keep repeating this over and over; if I did, he assured me, I would finally believe it.

When we had exchanged goodnights and Sam had turned out the light, I said my Hebrew prayer, Kria'th Shma. Then, having commended myself to God, I began repeating the litany, "There are no such things as ghosts." It worked. When I woke up to the sunny morning I had talked myself into believing it.

And I managed to believe it for two years, just as long as we lived at 584 High Street. In 1916 we moved to the new and bigger Schary Manor at No. 604 on the same street.

But when we did move I remember thinking how glad that lady ghost must be to get her house back again. Perhaps she had spared me because she had learned that I was a nice Jewish boy who had helped Mr. Gans in his hour of need.

3

Father Evens the Score with Max

The residents of High Street had a large number of expensive, or as we called them, high-class, automobiles. Young Louie Schwarz had a Stutz Bearcat, the Wosnitzers had a Pierce-Arrow, and other cars that chuffed down the street included a Lozier, a Hupmobile, Locomobile, Duesenberg and a Pope-Hartford (the most beautiful because it looked like a locomotive, which the Locomobile did not). There were also Franklins, Reos, Chevrolets, Roamers, and a Briscoe—a Cyclops among automobiles, with a single headlight smack in the middle of the radiator.

Years earlier my mother and father had given up their carriage and their horse, Jimmy. We all got around town by walking or by using the jitneys or trolley cars, which were a particular pleasure in spring and summer when the open-air models were put on the tracks. But as business flourished we had to have an "auto." Father couldn't afford one of the fancier types, so he settled for a black Maxwell touring car. But first he had to learn to drive. Sam was an expert driver, but he was married and living in New York. So Father took one or two lessons and then declared defiantly he was ready to take on the Maxwell. Needless to say, driving licenses in those days were dispensed far more casually than they are today.

From the beginning Pa looked upon the Maxwell as an enemy to be conquered. He believed that it could be controlled as readily and in the same way as his old horse Jimmy. Therefore he felt a sense of outrage when, on one of his first rides in the Maxwell, he stepped on the accelerator instead of the brake and was immediately propelled forward. The damn machine wasn't doing what he wanted it to do. Pa finally compromised by taking his foot off the gas and applying it to the brake. As the car shuddered to a halt, and in protest pressed Pa's stomach to the wheel, the vendetta was pledged.

For three days Pa refused to move the Maxwell out of the garage, a stable that had recently been converted. I can still remember the smell of the hay and manure and old leather harness that permeated our garage, though there had been no horse living there for over two years. I suspect that we happily ascribed animal characteristics to our first automobiles because they were substitutes for the pets we loved. I know that our family called this first car Max—all of us except Pa, that is, who referred to it only as "that damnation Maxwell."

One day Mother and Father had to fetch Zaida and Bubeh, who had been visiting Bubeh's sister. Mimeh (Aunt) Henya Hindman lived on Ferry Street, "down neck" in Newark. The section was called "down neck" because it led into the Plank Road, a wooden highway that in turn led to Jersey City and New York, and when traffic was heavy the horse carts and trucks and machines were bottlenecked there.

The visit to the Hindmans' vegetable store was uneventful. Mimeh Henya and her husband, Feter (Uncle) Dudy, gave us all tea, honey cake and apples, and then we started home. Father set the spark, cranked the Maxwell, and headed it down Hamburg Street (later renamed Wilson Street when we got into World War I).

Pa never stopped Max when he felt it wasn't truly called for, so he rolled along, blowing the horn to clear the way. Zaida, Bubeh and I sat in the back seat, motionless with fear. Occasionally Zaida would murmur, "*Meshugeneh*" (crazy one). Mother called out, "Hugo, look out!" or "Please, Hugo." With dogged determination, Pa plowed away, blowing the horn, alternately stepping on the gas and the brake, and murmuring curses at "that damnation Maxwell."

Finally we reached Washington Street, which was close to the foot of Court Street Hill, which wound up to High Street. The hill was the testing ground for all automobiles; owners boasted proudly when their machines could make the hill in high gear. You had a shred of dignity left if your car could make it in second gear, but many failed to get to the top except in first—and some could make it only if they got rid of their passengers. A police station at the foot of the hill restrained many daredevils eager to get a running start. Father used to go down Court Street Hill by carefully edging his way in first gear and sliding the foot brake to make sure that the Maxwell wouldn't get away from him. But he had always avoided the hill on the way home, returning by way of Springfield Avenue. On this day, however, he was determined to try it. He had to come to a dead stop at the bottom in order to let a brewery truck go by.

The car stalled. Father got out to crank it. Naturally, this held up traffic. A burly wagon driver tried to move his vehicle past the Maxwell, but because the space was too narrow, Father reached up, grabbed the bridle of the horse nearest him and brought it to a halt. The wagon driver roared, "What the hell are you doing?" Father answered politely, "If you don't mind, sir, there is traffic coming the other way, you see, so please wait, if you'll be so very kind."

When Mother heard this elaborate courtesy she was alarmed; it meant that Father was becoming angry, and she called out knowingly, "Please, Hugo, don't start a fight."

The wagon driver suggested that Father let go of the horses, and grabbed his whip.

Father said, "If you use that whip, I will take down your pants and give you a spanking."

I was able to see the wagon driver's face. He hesitated and looked at my father as if he couldn't believe what had been said. "What the hell did you say?" he asked.

My father said, "Please, my wife and mother-in-law are in the car, so do not curse. Be a gentleman . . ."

Luckily, just then a policeman from the First Precinct made his way across the street and told the wagon driver to back up his horses. Then he told Father to get into the car, spun the crank, Father waved him a salute and we started toward the hill. I looked back at the wagon driver, who still believed it was all a dream.

By now Father was racing along in second gear. As we gained speed he ground the car into high gear and we started up Court Street Hill. But it was a lost cause; we began to lose speed almost as soon as we hit the slope. Father shifted to second and we rallied briefly, but after another block we began to fade again. Bubeh became alarmed as we slowed down, and Father shifted into first gear. Then we began the slow crawl up the hill, with the Maxwell fighting Father's will all the way. Some fifty yards from the top it became clear that Max would never make it; Father secured the brakes and we came to a dead stop.

"What are you doing, Hugo?" my mother demanded.

"Belle, I'm not doing anything. Everybody has to get out and walk."

This was welcome news to Zaida and Bubeh, who got out of the car with alacrity. I followed, then helped my mother out of the front seat. Father waited until we were all clear; then with a roar of noise the Maxwell and he climbed the rest of the way.

At the top of the hill Father turned right to Schary Manor and pulled up smartly, with one wheel on the curb and the right front fender resting against a tree. As we walked toward him, we saw Father rush into the house.

Zaida and Bubeh went upstairs to rest and I followed Mother into the office, where we found Father talking to the man who had sold him the car. "Talking" is perhaps the wrong word. "You are, believe me, Gold-farb, a cheat. That car is a lemon, and if you don't give me a new one I'll drive down to your place and smash it in your window. Only a crook like you would do this to a brother Elk."

Apparently Goldfarb hung up, because Father said "Hello? Hello?," then hung up.

"Listen, Hugo, it isn't Goldfarb's fault. Why do you get so angry?" asked my mother.

Another of my father's peculiarities was that in moments of stress he had a soliloquy that he shared with a wall—any wall. In moments of torment or pique or disgust, when he felt that no one understood him, or didn't care to understand him, he would turn from the subject at hand and deliver a speech to the nearest wall.

Now he glared at the wall facing him. "Why do I get so angry, she asks me. I have to be a stick of wood. I have to let a man cheat me. I have to stick with a damnation machine and not say a word. What am I, wall, a man or a piece of wood?"

Mother sighed and started out of the room.

"My wife can't stand to hear me talk—"

I started out after Mother.

"—and my youngest son also is turning away from me."

"I'll stay, Pa," I said.

"Get out of here," he ordered.

I went.

Later that afternoon I was playing in front of the house with two of my friends, Frank Waxman and Milton Singer. My father came out and pushed the car off the curb. It settled onto the street with a groan. Then he set the spark, cranked it up and started down

High Street. A block away he made a U-turn and started back up High Street, headed west. I watched as he went by. Two blocks farther on he lost control of the car, ran up the curb and smashed it into the trunk of a large tree.

Frank, Milton and I ran toward the scene. As I ran, my eyes filled with tears; I saw myself an orphan. But long before we got to the car, Pa got out, kicked at Max viciously, wiped a spot of blood from his nose and started to walk toward us.

A neighbor called out, "Hey, Schary, are you hurt?"

My father answered, "Not me." He pointed at the car. "He is."

I trotted behind Pa. In the house he went straight to the telephone, ignoring my mother's frantic "What happened?" When he got Goldfarb on the phone Pa shouted, "Listen, Goldfarb, your rotten machine is on High Street in front of Doctor Hirschberg's house. You can use it for the junk yard. And don't ever say hello to me, because I wouldn't even spit on you." This time he was the one to hang up.

Two weeks later, Mother told me that we were getting a brand new Oldsmobile sedan. It seems that Goldfarb had retrieved the Maxwell, made up with my father and given him a good deal on a new car. But Pa never drove it. The trip in the Maxwell that day was the last time he ever drove a car. Max was dead and Pa was alive, and he intended to keep it that way.

So we got a chauffeur, whose name was Murray. The first ride Pa made him take was down Court Street Hill and then back up.

Murray, Pa and the Oldsmobile made it in high.

4

Mirror, Mirror, on the Wall

Each month when the electric bill arrived Papa would complain loud and long. "Look at this, look at the money we're spending for lights. A fortune. A family could live for a year in Kurland on what I have to pay each month for light." (Whenever Pa wanted to prove a point he would refer to Kurland, once a province of Germany, where he was born; things must have been wonderful in Kurland.) "But nobody cares until maybe there won't be bread in the house. Every night every light is burning like it was water and didn't cost. I talk my heart out, but who listens? Only the wall listens— but the wall don't burn lights . . ."

Father was almost intolerable on the subject of electric lights. If he left a room to answer the door, he'd turn out the light, knowing very well that he'd be returning within a few seconds. At night, if the family were alone and there was no affair being catered, every switch was flicked off except in the room in which we were gathered. When he poked his head into our room before going to sleep, he wouldn't say, "Go to sleep," he would yell, "Turn out the light." Each night he made a fast check before we went to bed, to make certain that all the lights were out in the kitchen, on the porch, in the lavatories, checkrooms and pantries. He would poke into every part of Schary Manor for a needlessly lighted bulb.

Then, when all of us were in our rooms Zaida would begin *his* nightly patrol.

Zaida had different motives. Papa was worried about lights; Zaida was worried about locks. Though he lived on the top floor in a room next to mine, where we were far removed from any burglars (who would have been satisfied with the table silver available in the basement), Zaida had a lifetime fear that "they" would come upon him and Bubeh and slaughter them. So each night after the last light was turned out, he would patter in his carpet slippers into the hall and down the steps on his nocturnal rounds to check all the locks on doors and windows. He never turned on the lights, however, because he didn't want to arouse Father.

Zaida knew each step, each landing and each door. He didn't wear pajamas; his nightclothes were his long underwear of whitish-gray wool with a drop seat. When I first saw Zaida in them he reminded me of a Dr. Denton baby with a gray beard.

Since by this time everyone was behind closed

doors, Zaida never bothered with a robe. When we heard the pat-pat of slippers, accompanied by the soft humming sound of a Jewish song, we knew that Zaida was on his way. First he would try the front door. It was always locked, but he would unlock it and lock it again, as if to tell us it wasn't properly secured in the first place. We could tell his progress by the sounds: "Zaida is at the front door"; "he's at the conservatory"; "now he's at the side door."

After a while there would be quiet (Zaida was somewhere in the basement), and then the pat-pat of the slippers would come up the steps, around the landing, up the steps, around the second landing and up more steps and into his bedroom. Finally there would be one more series of sounds: the closing of his door, the turning of the key in the door and the slipping of the bolt on a slide lock.

In all the years we lived in Schary Manor the only illegal entry was made by a drunk who fell against the glass door leading to the conservatory and was badly cut. Zaida's nightly tour was always the same, always uneventful, until the night after the mirror was installed in the hall.

The steps leading from the conservatory to the second floor ended on a wide landing, off which were my parents' and sisters' bedrooms and two rooms for boarders who lived in Schary Manor. These boarders were usually rich and retired people who liked Mother's cooking and our rather luxurious quarters. Also off this landing was a room and bathroom used by the bride and her entourage before the wedding. Later she would return to change into the inevitable suit and hat for the honeymoon dash down the steps, through the volleys of rice, and into the car that coughed away with clanking cans and a "Just Married" sign.

There was one long wall on this landing that Papa had originally decorated with wallpaper murals that were very out-doorsy, very French—and very much. The wall was about nine feet high and fifteen feet long, and one day Papa got an idea. He decided to cover the whole wall with a mirror. Entire wedding processions could stand before it to check their costumes and poses; it would be functional, and one more example of Schary Manor's special service and care.

Workmen stripped the wall of its French mural two days before the mirror was due. But a difficulty arose: how to get a nine-foot mirror through a seven-foot door? The matter was solved by Papa, who moved the entire crew to the driveway, which ran past the conservatory. Two French doors were dismantled, and after loud commands and countercommands the mirror was up the landing and against the wall. There were acres of mirror, and the installation was complicated but accomplished with remarkably little fuss. Papa held his temper in check for fear that the mirror would break.

After the day's work was done and the workmen, well stuffed with beer and Father's congratulations, had all gone, Rosie Carter and the kitchen girls cleaned the mirror and swept and scrubbed the entire landing. The whole family stood in front of it, adoring it and our own images. There seemed to be so many of us. We laughed at it, made faces, hopped and swayed and then posed as if for a family photograph. Father looked triumphant, Mother proud, Lillian insouciant, Frances a bit embarrassed, and I smug (I thought the mirror made me look taller). Zaida only glanced at it; he was too orthodox a Jew to preen in front of a mirror. But Bubeh stood for a moment and smiled, as if America were too much for her to understand.

"Did you ever see such a beautiful mirror?" Papa said.

None of us ever had.

Mother had a worry. "If anyone fell against it, he could kill himself."

"That won't happen—and anyway we've got insurance," said Pa.

Lillian said that it would be a help to her, for she could rehearse her songs for the Y.M.H.A. show in front of it.

"I didn't get this mirror so you should go to Proctor's Palace and be on the stage with tramps," Papa warned her.

"There's nothing wrong with Belle Baker or the Courtney Sisters. They're not tramps," Lillian protested.

Father turned on her, and in a moment the mirror held the reflection of him yelling at Lillian, Lillian yelling back, Mother moving between them, Frances pulling at Father's arm trying to calm him down, and me looking frightened, because I was sure that Lillian was going to get slapped and perhaps me too. But it was Bubeh who saved the day when she shouted, "Look—look!" She pointed to the mirror. "Is that what you want the mirror to see, Hugo, on its first day? Look—"

We looked. The tension disappeared, and we went to our rooms to get ready for the evening's work.

It was a normal wedding celebration: the ceremony was at eight-thirty instead of seven-thirty; there were twenty extra guests; the orchestra played "Oh, Promise

Me" a half-tone off pitch; the groom's brother drank too much too quickly and was sick before dinner; Father lost his temper when the guests banged the dishes with the silver during the speeches; and the master of ceremonies read the usual series of telegrams:

"May your life be as bright as Luna Park at night."

"May all your troubles be little ones."

"May you have a smooth journey on the sea of matrimony."

"Sorry cannot be with you. Signed, President Wilson."

"Regret my plans keep me overseas. Signed, General Pershing."

At one o'clock in the morning the orchestra scratched away at "Goodnight, Ladies," and Lillian and I finished checking out the hats and coats. The checkroom was Lillian's domain, but I was beginning to muscle in and Lillian gave me a third of the take.

Then the family sat down in the kitchen for the customary *schmoos* (relaxed, unhurried conversation, rambling, gossipy and uninhibited) and late snack of rye bread, scrambled eggs, cream cheese and coffee and milk. The ladies talked about the dresses, Father talked about the bad manners of some of the guests, and Zaida complained about the ceremony. He always thought that Rabbi Brodsky's conventional conclusion, "Now kiss your bride and be happy," was too waggish for an orthodox wedding. On this particular evening we also talked about the new mirror. It had been a smashing success; guests had climbed the steps all evening to look at it and themselves.

Finally the kitchen staff went home and the family went to bed. Father turned out the lights as we pro-

ceeded from one area of the house to another, barely
giving us time to enter the next pool of light.

In my room I counted out my earnings (substantial
—over seven dollars), then undressed and crawled into
bed. The house was quiet, and I waited for the sound of
Zaida to begin his tour. In a few minutes I heard his
door open, then his footfalls as he went down the steps,
then the sounds of the locks being tested. After a while
I heard him coming upstairs from the conservatory.
There was silence, then some mumbled words I couldn't
distinguish, another spell of silence, and finally a laugh.
This irregularity in Zaida's routine puzzled me, so I got
out of bed, slipped into my robe and headed for the
landing. By now other doors were opening, lights were
being turned on (much to Father's annoyance), and
soon the entire family were gathered on the second floor
listening to Zaida tell us what had happened.

Zaida had walked his usual route, finished lock-
ing-up and then gone up the steps leading to the second
floor. Suddenly there appeared in front of him a figure
in white. Zaida took a step forward and the figure
moved to meet him. Zaida halted. So did the ghostly
figure.

Zaida called softly, *"Ver's duh?"* (Who's there?)

No answer. Again he advanced, and again the
figure moved toward him. Now Zaida abandoned his
Yiddish and called louder, "Who's there?" Still no
answer. By now he was on the landing, and so was the
figure.

Zaida prepared to meet his destiny. The two approached each other. Only as Zaida got close enough to
reach out and touch the apparition—who was also reach-
ing out with his hands—did he remember that the mirror

had been installed in the hallway and that he was standing in front of it. He peered at his own image, tall and
erect in his underwear and skull cap and slippers. He
nodded and greeted himself. "Hello, Baruch," he said,
and then laughed.

By the time Zaida had finished his story the house
was bursting with light and laughter. His experience
set off a string of stories by my mother and father and
Bubeh. We didn't get to bed until after three. Before I
fell asleep I heard Zaida close his door, turn the lock,
slip the bolt and laugh once more with delight as Bubeh
called out mockingly, "Who's there?"

Thereafter when one of us approached or crossed in
front of that mirror we'd steal a look and say, "Hello,
Baruch."

5

Zaida versus the United States Army

It wasn't that Zaida was not a patriot—he loved the United States. But to Zaida anybody in uniform was a Cossack. If the mailman, on a rainy day, delivered letters that were a bit damp, he was a Cossack. The milkman, clinking bottles too noisily, was a Cossack. Though he had served a three-year stint in service as a tuba player in a Russian regiment, Zaida regarded uniforms as a mark of unworthy authority. Therefore policemen, firemen, liveried chauffeurs, the U.S. Army, and all the rest of the uniformed brigade of citizens were Cossacks. Further, the Army wasn't kosher.

In the spring of 1918 High Street was a wide and well-paved residential thoroughfare that had no street-car tracks and no jitney service. Huge truck convoys carrying troops and materiel up from Camp Dix to embarkation areas in Hoboken and Weehawken would occasionally back up into Newark, and High Street was selected for temporary bivouac because it was away from the stream of traffic yet provided a direct route to main arteries. The trees were shady, there were no saloons, pool halls or other commercial attractions, and it was quiet.

One late afternoon, a Thursday, a long line of brown trucks appeared and parked on both sides of High Street. Soldiers popped out wearing their helmets and cartridge belts and carrying bayonets, and soon we are all part of the war effort. Neighbors appeared with cold lemonade, cookies and sandwiches. The girls prettied up and we young boys swaggered along hoping that the soldiers watching us saunter by, thirteen years tall, would wonder why fine strapping lads like us weren't in the Army winning the war.

I was standing outside when I became aware of a group of officers moving up the steps to our outer porch. Sensing that this was to be my call to service, I rushed over in time to see my father greet the visitors. The Colonel in charge was a lean, lantern-jawed gentleman with a soft voice. He had seen our sign, "Schary Manor, Catering," and he asked permission for the Army cooks to use our kitchens for the soldiers' evening meal.

"Certainly, gentlemen, certainly," my father assured them, shaking each one by the hand and making them welcome. As he showed them into the house he managed a casual salute.

One look at the tide of khaki-clad figures brought forth an explosive "Cossacks!" from Zaida; taking Bubeh by the hand, he retreated to his rooms on the top floor.

But Zaida had curiosity and perfect hearing, and when the voices of the visitors did not go away, he made his reappearance, apparently ready to fight for Bubeh's honor against the threat of the invaders. By now huge men were bringing in big trays and pans and stores of food. Our kitchen staff was helping the Army cooks light our huge wood and coal stoves that extended the length of the longest wall in the kitchen. These solid black ranges were cemented to the wall, with the sides and tops bolted to the backs. They had browned, baked, boiled, roasted and fried thousands of chickens, fish, potatoes, squab and asparagus, and had delivered them and other delicacies piping hot to guests in our strictly kosher catering establishment.

Into the kitchen marched Zaida, his skull cap set squarely on top of his head, his jaw set squarely under his gray square beard. His blue eyes darted about, cataloguing each detail. One soldier murmured a hello; Zaida ignored him, then turned around and walked out. I ran after him and took his hand; he pressed it tightly and pulled me along through the pantry, through the lower hall and up the steps to the office.

"What's the matter, what's the matter, Zaida?"

Zaida only said, "Shut up." He yanked me into the office, pushed me to one side, shut the door behind him and faced my father, mother, and Bubeh, who had sneaked down to see what was going on.

"What's the matter, Totta [Father]?" Mother asked.

This time Zaida was more explicit. "Cossacks," he said.

My father rose and prepared to deliver a stirring address. "Totta," he said, "these are soldiers who are fighting for you and me."

"They don't have to do me any favors," said Zaida.

Father started once again. "Totta—"

Zaida cut in. "Do you know what's going on downstairs there? Ham and bacon is going on. This house is *treyf;* it is defiled. May the good Lord have mercy on all of us."

Bubeh groaned. The meat kitchen was her pride and joy. Now the flesh of the pig was desecrating it. My mother also groaned and looked at my father. "Hugo, what can we do—what can we do?"

Father was as meticulous as they about running a kosher place, but there was a war and he was determined to be a patriot. Because he had been born in Kurland, Father often spoke *hoch Deutsch* (High German), and his manners were courtly, as befitted an upper-middle-class German. But when the United States declared war, Father had given up his German and only used Yiddish or Polish in his conversations with Zaida. In his daily conversations with the rest of the community he had even eliminated *Gesundheit;* when acknowledging a sneeze, he would nod and say, "Bless you."

Being very self-conscious about the German heritage of which he had been so proud, Father now had to disassociate himself from all things Hunnish. He was the first to buy war bonds, and Schary Manor flew a flag each day, and even at night, until we were told it wasn't correct to do so. Father was one of the first Newarkers to know all the verses to "Over There," and he made the orchestra play the song at every bar mitzvah and wedding.

Therefore Father had a special feeling about the Army using Schary Manor. It would make for good off-hand talk at the next pinochle game: "The Colonel is a very respectable gentleman, and I told him that my house and all that is in it is at the service of the United States and President Wilson." Father always got President Wilson into the conversation because he had often been told that he resembled the President; his face was oblong, his teeth long and prominent, and he wore pince-nez. (The resemblance also solidified his Democratic political convictions.)

For all these reasons Papa spoke up firmly and calmly—at first. "Belle," he said to my mother, "there is nothing to do. God isn't crazy and He knows we are doing nothing wrong. God in His wisdom is smarter than your father."

"*Chochem,*" snorted Zaida. This term is roughly translatable as "wise guy."

"What should I do?" Now Father was beginning to raise his voice. "What should I do?" Then a note higher, "What should I *do!* Throw them out? Tell the United States Army my father-in-law don't want them dirtying the kitchen? Is that what I should do?"

"No, Hugo, no," my mother comforted him.

"*Nu,* then should I tell them I'm a German sympathizer and disgrace all of us? Should my neighbors call me a spy?"

Zaida had a helpful suggestion. "Don't be a damn fool, Hugo."

My father looked at the wall behind him. It was one of those times when no living person was able to understand him, so he presented his logic to the wall. "Wall, do you hear? I'm not smart enough to talk sense to my wife or my father-in-law—who is the world's most pious Jew—so I'll talk to you. You can hear me, wall. We understand each other. So, listen, wall, tell my father-in-law that this is Schary Manor. It carries the name of Herman Hugo Schary and it belongs to me, and if I want the Army to use our kosher kitchen, it's my decision, my kitchen, my house and my office. You hear me, wall?"

By the time he turned around to face Zaida, the old gentleman had gone downstairs back to the kitchen, taking Bubeh with him. My mother nodded mock approval as my father turned to her. "Very good, Hugo. It was a nice speech for your youngest son."

Papa looked at me, then back to Mama. "It won't hurt him. When he grows up he'll maybe have enough sense to be boss in his own house." He started for the door. "Besides," he added as an exit line, "war is war."

I had only one thing on my mind. I asked, "Is Zaida right? Will God punish us?"

"I don't think so." Mother sighed, smiled and kissed me. "Believe me, Sonny, sometimes I worry more about your father than I do about God."

I went downstairs with Mother to see what Zaida and Bubeh were doing. In the kitchen the stoves were roaring, and the smell of bacon grease hung over the air as if challenging the ghostly smells of noodle soup, gefilte fish and strudel. Zaida was standing in a corner; in front of him, seated in a chair, was Bubeh. Mother didn't want them to stay, but Zaida insisted that Bubeh remain. He, however, would go to his room and pray. "Stay, Shaina; watch them," he said to Bubeh. "Watch everything they do. When the Cossacks go, I'll be back." On that note he departed.

Some time later the troops queued up in the driveway for their supper. They moved into our kitchen with mess plates and come out with steaming piles of beans and potatoes and ham and bacon and chunks of hot bread. One of the soldiers offered me some of his food, but I knew Zaida must be watching from somewhere so I managed to resist the offer. After dinner some of the soldiers began to sing. An improvised block party got under way, with Laura Fineberg and my sister Lillian acting as leaders of the social.

Then at about ten o'clock soldiers on motorcycles appeared. Orderlies began to move about, a bugle blew, and almost as suddenly as they had appeared, the convoy was on its way to Hoboken. We all waved good-bye and my father led us in singing all the verses to "Over There." The soldiers sang back as they rolled off to the war in France.

The residents of High Street chatted for a while. Father told some of the neighbors about his personal conversations with the Colonel, and then the neighbors slowly drifted home. The lights began to dim on the Great Adventure. When Father and I got home, we went looking for the rest of the family. They were all in the kitchen—Zaida, Bubeh, Mother, Lillian, my older sister, Frances, Rosie Carter and John, the head janitor. With them were five kitchen helpers recruited by Rosie and the staff of four janitors and porters assembled by John. My mother was translating Zaida's instructions into action.

"Build fires in the yard. Fill the soup kettles with water. Get the wrenches and take the stoves apart. Get hot water and brushes and the kosher scrubbing soap."

Father asked feebly, "What's going on?" but no one listened. He knew very well what was going on, and he decided to see that it was done properly. Now that the Army was gone the kosher kitchen had to be restored. Father had the strongest arms in the house, so he grabbed the first wrench and loosened the first bolt. In the back yard, fires were built and Zaida helped John construct the tripods to hold the huge kettles. As the ranges were disassembled the pieces were brought into the yard and deposited in the boiling water with ice tongs. Rosie and the other girls scrubbed Rokeach kosher soap over the iron sections as Zaida intoned Hebrew prayers of devotion and cleanliness. When I asked what he was saying, he told me to shut up and go to bed.

As the prayers continued and the sections of the stove were cleaned, they were taken back to the kitchen, where Father and John and the porters replaced them. Meanwhile Bubeh and Mother and my sisters were scrubbing the serving tables and the floors and the walls. Every few minutes Zaida would come in to check on the proceedings and say an appropriate blessing.

It was dawn when the job was done. Bubeh and Mother made coffee and scrambled eggs and everybody sat down in the kitchen. Before we ate, Zaida blessed the food. Once again the smell of coffee and milk and fresh fried butter filled the room.

"*Nu*," said my father, "it wasn't so bad. We helped the Army and everything is kosher again and God is satisfied, and maybe even Zaida."

Zaida looked up from his saucer, then drained the rest of the coffee. "It's time already for morning prayers." He got up and walked out of the kitchen, his skull cap pushed to one side at a rakish angle. There was a look of triumph about him.

My father's voice pursued him. "It was a good night's work, Totta."

Zaida stopped and said, "Hugo, it's your house, your office and your kitchen. But let me tell you something, *chochem,* those were my prayers. Goodnight, everybody."

We all laughed and then I fell asleep at the table and Papa carried me to bed.

6

Yom Kippur Should Never Come on a Weekday

The synagogue which my family attended was the Anshe Russia. It was an orthodox temple, presided over by Rabbi Brodsky, a tall patriarch with a long, flowing Old Testament beard. He had skin which looked like new white parchment, and his hands moved like flying doves. The holiday and regular Friday-night and Saturday-morning services were held in the large praying hall; weekday-morning services (Shacharis) and nightly services (Maariv) were held in the small cellar-like room below the main sanctuary.

Once in a while during the week I would call for Zaida at the synagogue and walk home with him. While waiting I would sit in the small room and listen to the men pray. They were all expert and devoted, and they rattled through their *davening* (praying) in firm, clear voices. I didn't understand any of the prayers, couldn't read a word of Hebrew at that time except for the letters on butcher shops which spelled "Kosher," and had no knowledge of why certain things were done in our home. If I asked Zaida he would only answer, "Don't ask questions. Just do it."

Sometimes Father would tell me something about the holidays, but early in life I began to suspect that he wasn't quite as knowledgeable about Judaism as he was supposed to be. Mother told me that I mustn't think of God as a person. She explained that the phrase "God made man in His image" meant that we were the image God had of man, but that God wasn't necessarily *like* man. But with so many references to "the Hand of God" and "the Voice of God," it was a losing battle not to think of God as a man. It was much like being told not to think of a rhinoceros while making the magic formula for gold. Not until I was well into my twenties was I able to believe deeply in God without visualizing him.

Many times my friends and I talked about God, but in those days our conversation related mainly to our fear of Him. Having been raised in orthodox homes, we were told that we mustn't eat dairy food with meat dishes, mustn't eat or drink at all on Yom Kippur, mustn't eat bread or forbidden food during the Passover holiday, must *never* eat pig or shellfish at any time. Most of our religion at that age had to do with denying ourselves food. We all believed that to break the dietary laws was to call down the wrath of God's displeasure upon us; we would either choke on the forbidden food or be struck with a terrible disease, like little Irving

Weinstein, who had to be pushed in a wheel chair and would never walk.

Yom Kippur, the Day of Atonement, was always the most solemn day of the Jewish year. It came eight days after the beginning of the New Year and our families approached this day of fasting with sturdy resolution. We had heard stories of Jews who actually didn't fast the entire day, but we knew that this must be a lie. It was inconceivable to think of a Jew brash enough to defy the Law of God.

When Jewish boys become thirteen they have their bar mitzvah, and one of the responsibilities they assume is to fast on Yom Kippur. At that age they are considered old enough to understand the traditional vows and to assume the obligations of Judaism. My first Yom Kippur came only a few weeks after my thirteenth birthday, and I girded myself for the ordeal. I told all my friends that it would be no hardship, but I was convinced that by the end of the twenty-four hours without food or water I would be in critical condition. Doctors would try in vain to restore my health and I would be remembered as a martyr to true faith.

As Yom Kippur Eve drew near, I bathed and dressed in a clean shirt and a new blue suit that my parents had bought me for my bar mitzvah. Mother told me to wear a maroon tie. Ever since, when I wear a blue suit, white shirt and red tie, I remember my thirteenth birthday. It was a Tuesday night and, though I didn't dare confess it, I was pleased that on Wednesday I would not have to go to school.

We had a typical Yom Kippur Eve supper: chicken soup and roast chicken, both lightly seasoned in order to cut down our need for liquid, and sponge cake and tea—lots of tea. By sundown the food was finished and we were all off for *shul*. Each man carried his velvet bag containing his *talis* (prayer shawl) and *yarmalke*. The ladies walked with us to temple and went upstairs to the gallery reserved for them.

Zaida, Father and I all sat together. I recited the proper prayer before putting on my *talis,* then kissed it and placed it over my shoulders. Already I felt thirsty.

On Yom Kippur, Zaida wore his huge black and white praying shroud, the one in which he would be buried. Many members of the congregation, including Zaida, slipped off their shoes and put on slippers, for they had hours of prayer ahead of them that evening and the whole of the next day until sunset. Much of that time they would be on their feet, and they tried to make themselves as comfortable as possible for the ordeal. Rabbi Brodsky, beautifully robed and with a stunning white satin crown that looked like a chef's hat, began the Kol Nidre service. Yom Kippur had begun. By this time I knew I would die of hunger before morning.

The excitement of the event dwindled after twenty minutes. Because I couldn't read Hebrew well I didn't know what the words meant, and it seemed that we were always rising just a moment after we'd sat down. Father and Zaida were oblivious of me, and I was conscious of the peculiar smell of the Anshe Russia temple. It was comprised of talcum powder, snuff, hair tonic, camphor, and the musty odor of old prayer books.

It was a warm night and the whole congregation had turned out, including the walking sick and ailing. There was a good deal of coughing and sneezing, which added a noisy background to the murmurs of the congregation, all of whom were qualified, if necessary, to stand on the *bimah* (platform) and conduct the service. They knew all the prayers, all the chants, and they could read from the Torah. They did not pray in unison. Some of them took their own sweet time; others, caught by the rhythm of the prayers, rushed along in a faster tempo. Every once in a while one of the congregants would go into business for himself. He would burst into loud prayer, addressing himself to God in a voice that was certain to be heard above all others. No one minded.

After some time I looked into the gallery. Mother was smiling down at me; I waved to her and she nodded. My sisters were with her and they both looked bored stiff; they had come along for the walk. Bubeh was reading her *siddur* (prayer book) but took time out to nod to me when Mother nudged her.

The getting-up and sitting-down continued and the incessant praying went on and on. I knew I wasn't required to stay for the entire service; my mother was to signal me when it was time to go. I kept looking back at her until Zaida became annoyed. "*Genug,*" he said, "enough," and gave me a slight shove. I crept out, met my mother and sisters in the lobby, and we walked home.

By bedtime my throat was as dry as sand. For a moment I played with the idea of feigning illness (a person very old or sick was not allowed to fast). I knew I could fool my mother, maybe even Zaida when he got home, but I also knew that I'd have a rough time with God and I gave up the idea. Much to my astonishment I woke up the next morning in a good state of health. In the same holiday clothes I started out to temple by myself. Father and Zaida had risen hours before and were already at their devotions. Mother and my sisters kissed me goodbye; they were all fasting but were not going to temple until late in the day, just in time for the finish. Apparently women were not saddled with the same demands made upon us men.

As I walked to temple I thought about the feast with which we broke the fast. First of all there would be sliced oranges, then some marinated herring and hot coffee and tea. Then, after an appropriate wait, the real supper would begin. The food made the day before would be heated for the evening meal. It would be a large family affair; all the aunts and uncles and cousins would be there (they were always there for holidays and Friday-night dinners), and there would be singing and jokes. It would be a real Yom Tov, a great holiday—if I lasted the day. But I had some doubts. I was languishing with thirst and my body was wasting away from lack of nourishment.

Outside the temple I met Harold Lasser, a close friend, who had been born thirty days before me. He was taking his fast just about as well as I. We talked for a while, but finally Harold said that talking only made one more thirsty, and left me to sit in the sun in front of the temple. I went in to say good morning to Zaida and my father. Pa wanted to know how I was bearing up; I told him manfully I was quite sure I could make it, but I said it in tones that would leave him in no doubt that it was going to be a heroic accomplishment. Zaida shrugged and told me that in a little

while I'd also be allowed to fast on Tisha Ba'Ab, another holy day. I hadn't heard of Tisha Ba'Ab before;
I felt it should not have been sprung on me as a surprise.

I stayed in temple until about noon, then went out
to get some air. The lobby was crowded with members
of the congregation taking time out, and so many of
them asked me how I was bearing up that I strolled
away up Kinney Street.

There was a public school on Kinney Street near
Belmont Avenue. It was lunch time. Many young
Christians were aware of and resentful of the fact
that their Jewish schoolmates were getting an extra
day off because of the holy day. Some of them would
run past the temple screaming insults, but these were
usually the bigger boys and the fastest runners. They
were gone before anyone could answer or retaliate.
Without realizing it, I was soon quite a distance from
the safety of my *shul*. A group of young men moved up
to me. They wanted to know if I was a Jew; they said
I looked like one, I dressed like one, I even smelled like
one. One of them pinched me; when I jumped, another
flipped out my tie. "Hey, sheeny matzoh, look at me,"
said another. As I looked he spat at me; when I spat
back one of them hit me.

After that I was too scared to know what I was
doing, but I must have hit back, for I found myself on
the pavement being pummeled and kicked. My shirt
was torn and some dirt was thrown at me. Finally some
of the older men from the temple came up the hill,
and the boys ran away. I was helped to my feet; someone wiped my bleeding nose. I pulled away, ashamed
and hurt. All I wanted was to be alone, and when some-

one offered to call my father, I said no and started to run home.

In those days I used to think I could run forever. I was short for my age and seemed to be tireless. When I got to Schary Manor, sweating, crying and bleeding, I ran into the house past my sisters and up the steps into my room. Mother and Lillian and Frances followed me. Frances got some water and Mother and Lillian took off my torn clothes. Lillian wanted to leave immediately and go to the Belmont Avenue school and kill somebody, anybody. (Lillian defended all members of her family. In the old days, during the gang fights on Thirteenth Avenue, she would wield a broomstick or a baseball bat; once she knocked down a drunk who was trying to pull Zaida's beard.)

Mother told me to take a drink of water, but by now I wasn't thirsty. Also I was stubborn; all I agreed to do was to take a nap. Lillian and Frances left the room and Mother sat down next to me. I asked her why those boys had acted that way; I was feeling very sorry for myself. After all, this had happened while I was in the middle of a religious sacrifice. It seemed like a raw deal, and the sum and substance of my complaint was that I didn't deserve it.

Mother pointed out that the punishments we deserved were of little value. "After all," she said, "when you do something wrong, you know you'll get punished. So you say, 'Nu, I deserved it. It wasn't so bad. It was worth it.' Or maybe you say, 'Nu, I won't do that again.' One way or the other, you know you had it coming to you—like a bellyache when you eat too much. But when you get something bad that you don't deserve, if you learn to take that without being a real baby, then you become a real grown-up person. It makes you a *mensch* —a person."

That made sense. I felt put-upon, but I also resolved to be manly about it.

When I awoke it was almost sunset, and I dressed and prepared to go to *shul*. Before leaving, Mother had told Rosie Carter that I was to wait for them at home, but I decided to behave as if nothing had happened. On my way I met Mother and Father, who were bound for home. Father leaned down and hugged me and wished me a good year. Then we all walked back to Schary Manor together.

As the sun set, Zaida and Bubeh came home and the relatives began to arrive: Aunt Mae and Uncle Mike, Aunt Jennie and Uncle Eppie, and all the rest of the tribe. The tables were spread with light food to break the fast, and we waited patiently for Zaida to finish washing and recite the prayer of thanksgiving so that we could begin. The conversation was quick and happy. As I told my cousins of the attack made upon me, the extent of my injuries kept multiplying, though all I could exhibit was a slight swelling on my nose.

One of my uncles suggested that the moral of my sad tale was that Yom Kippur should never come on a weekday. Finally Zaida came into the room and called me to his side. Since this was my first Yom Kippur, he wanted me to recite the prayer of thanks to God.

I broke a piece of bread, sprinkled it with salt, and recited the grace. When I finished, everyone called out, "*Mazeltov*" (good luck, congratulations). I looked at Mother and we smiled at each other.

7

The Spanish Influenza

When we first heard about the Spanish Influenza in 1918 it sounded like a dread foreign disease. But we believed that it would gain little foothold in healthy American soil. We never referred to it as "the flu" or "influenza," but always in somber tones as *The Spanish Influenza,* spoken as if in italics.

During the war I sold Liberty bonds and thrift stamps on the corner of Broad and Market streets. At the time, this was proudly identified by Newarkers as the busiest intersection in America. A few of us extroverted thirteen-year-olds would mount a small wooden platform and sing songs and plead with the passers-by to buy bonds.

Everybody was doing something to help the Allies.

Frances and Lil used to go to Hoboken to pass out doughnuts and coffee to the soldiers going to France. My brother Sam was one of the Minute-Men who spoke in theatres and sold Liberty bonds. I once went to hear him speak in Proctor's Palace. Sam told the story of the Negro driver who, being adept with his whip, used it to kill bothersome bees on his horse's rump. But when he was asked to snap his whip at a beehive to prove his marksmanship, he answered, "No, suh, they's organized."

"When the Kaiser struck poor Belgium, that was one bee; poor France was another; but when he struck America, he hit a beehive," my brother concluded, with a thrust of his fist and his voice loud with excitement. The audience stormed approval and Mr. Louis Bamberger bought a fifty-thousand-dollar bond.

Mother and Bubeh knitted socks and mufflers and sweaters for the Red Cross. Father bought bonds, sent food to the hospitals and camps, and stopped speaking German. Along with other Safety Cadets at the Morton Street school, I distributed copies of *The Stars and Stripes,* marched in countless parades, and put all my checkroom tips in thrift stamps and Liberty bonds.

But what I liked best—because it was the most fun—was singing to my fellow citizens at Broad and Market streets. The first song, which acted as an effective ice-breaker and was always sung in chorus, went this way:

> For your boy and my boy,
> And all the boys out there,
> Let's lend our money for the U.S.A.
> And do our share.

Every bond that we are buying
Will help hold the fighting line.
Buy Bonds, Buy Bonds—buy bonds for your
    boy and mine.

If Lillian wasn't busy working in theatres, her rich
contralto would lead the chorus. I also did two solos.
One went:

Goodbye Ma,
Goodbye Pa,
Goodbye mule with your old hee-haw.
I don't know what this war's about
But you bet, by gosh, I'll soon find out.
And my sweetheart, don't you fear
I'll bring you a King for a souvenir.
I'll bring you a Turk and a Kaiser, too,
And that's about all one fella can do.

My gestures for that song were obvious but effective, and usually I got a generous response. But I didn't
wait too long, under any circumstances, to get into my
second number:

Keep your head down, Fritzie Boy

        .   .   .   .   .

You were fixing your barbed wire
When we opened rapid fire.
If you want to see your Fadder in
    der Fadderland
Keep your head down, Fritzie Boy.

This one usually brought the biggest hand, and
I'd follow it with a speech about the boys who were
fighting "over there," and that all we had to do here
at home was to keep on buying bonds and stamps. I

was so obviously sincere that the money kept clanking into the big barrel near the platform, and the girls at the tables set up in front of the Fireman's Insurance Building were kept busy selling.

Lil also had a couple of specialties. She sang "The Rose of No Man's Land" in a way that broke your heart, and when she urged the audience to join us in the crashing finale of "Over There," we sometimes stopped traffic.

As a result of our efforts Lil and I were asked to appear at war rallies in public halls and auditoriums, and sometimes we even went into Army camps and hospitals nearby to do our act. On such occasions I would wear a helmet and a cartridge belt and the canvas leggings of the period, and I loved every minute of it. Lil was such a success that she was catapulted into leading singing roles at the Y.M.H.A. shows and had dreams of a career in the theatre—a prospect that made Pa furious whenever it was mentioned. But since these performances were part of the war effort, he permitted her to continue, always reserving the right to choke off her career once the Boches were defeated.

One evening in late September of 1918, after Yom Kippur, Lil and I made an appearance in a drizzling rain at Broad and Market streets. When I came home I told Mother that I was chilly. She felt my cheeks, put me to bed and called Dr. Nash, who arrived on the double, and after examining his now hot and shivery patient, whispered to my mother that I had *The Spanish Influenza*. I felt like a war casualty and wondered if the family would be entitled to put a Gold Star in the window if I weren't strong enough to fight off the dreaded fever.

But after a few days Dr. Nash's work and Mother's *kraftik* (strong) chicken soup knocked the feeble germs out of me and I felt well again. I was kept home for a few more days, however, on the advice of Grace Lewis, a sturdy lady who was living in our house as a boarder. Grace was authoritative and firm. She was working around the clock driving army ambulances and making speeches at bond rallies and had only come home for some fresh laundry. When she heard I'd been ill, she left strict orders. "Keep him in. This disease is awful. If you get it a second time before you're over the first attack, you're finished." Mother was convinced and I was scared stiff; I nursed my weak body with infinite care. But soon it was clear that I was completely well and could no longer be pampered.

The schools had been shut down because of the growing epidemic, and each day brought additional bulletins of the sick and dying and dead. We learned that *The Spanish Influenza* was killing more soldiers than German bullets. One of the Hollander boys had died of the illness in an Army camp, many of our friends were coming down with it, and there was a growing sense of panic. But what really convinced me of the potency of the sickness was the news that Grace Lewis had been hit by it and was in the hospital. If it could successfully attack Grace Lewis it must be a very powerful germ.

Then one morning Frances took ill with extraordinary suddenness. She was eating breakfast, when inexplicably she fainted. After we got her upstairs we learned that Aunt Anna, who hadn't yet come down for breakfast, was also feverish. Mother took one look and knew that we now had two new patients.

The call went out to the ubiquitous Dr. Nash, but he was so busy with other patients that he didn't get to Schary Manor until early afternoon. By then Zaida and Bubeh were victims, along with our porter, John, who greeted the illness with his expression for every occasion, "Sonamonbitch." Dr. Nash gave Mother and Lillian orders while I ran to the drugstore for the prescriptions and for rubbing alcohol, cotton, hot water bottles, enema bags and camphor oil.

By that night Mother was ill, and Father took care of her while Lil and I tended the others. Rosie Carter, our huge and competent handymaid, announced loftily that she was going to ignore the stupid sickness; she simply refused to become sick and proceeded to take over as cook and bottle-washer.

In the morning Father took sick. Because he was so huge and there was so much more of his sickness to contend with, we shifted Mother to Lil's room and left Father alone in his and Mother's bed. Zaida was using my room, and Lil and I bedded down on mattresses in the third-floor hall.

When Dr. Nash called, he was dismayed to find that his list of patients had burgeoned to such an extent. He made a few frantic calls for nurses, but this was like shouting into the wind. What few healthy nurses there were had been recruited for hospitals and for private homes where disaster had struck earlier. As Dr. Nash was telling Lillian and me how to handle the situation, Rosie called us. She had taken lunch up to Mrs. Goetz, another boarder in the house, and found her ill. Mrs. Goetz was an elderly lady, the widow of a rich man, who had moved in with us because she liked Mother and her cooking. Being a diabetic, she needed special food and attention, and she insisted that we call her own doctor, who knew her diabetic condition in detail. Dr. Nash seemed to be relieved that at least she was not going to be his responsibility.

When he left, Lil and I sat down with Rosie Carter and totted up the score.

Mother was in Lil's room.

Frances was in her own room.

Father was in his room.

Aunt Anna was in her room.

Zaida was in my room.

Bubeh was in her room.

Mrs. Goetz was in her room.

John was in his room.

Luckily, the Kridels, also boarders, had gone to Florida. Grace Lewis was sick in the hospital, and Mr. Londau, our last boarder, was in Washington, D.C., working for the Jewish Welfare Board. Still, we had eight patients—four on the third floor, four on the fourth floor—all of whom had to be fed.

For a mad moment Lil thought of turning one of the banquet rooms on the second floor into a catchall infirmary. But she rejected the idea almost as soon as she mentioned it; the picture of Aunt Anna, Mrs. Goetz, Frances, John, Mother, Father, Zaida and Bubeh all viewing each other's misery was too ridiculous.

We arranged a schedule. Rosie would stay in the kitchen, make the food, and take care of John. Lil would be on the third floor and I on the fourth. If one of us had to go down to the kitchen for ice, water or food, the other would patrol both areas.

By now I knew I wasn't going to get that second attack, but I was worried about Lil. She and Rosie were the only ones who hadn't been struck down. I believed Rosie when she said she had no intention of letting "that *Spanish Influenza* put me down," but I was less confident of Lil's boast, "I never get sick."

All day the two of us tramped the halls and steps, bringing food and administering medicine and giving massages. We slept in shifts. Lil had a huge alarm clock which we kept in the hall to remind us of our hourly tours of duty. The first time it went off it was so loud that it woke all the patients as well as Lil. Thereafter she muffled it with a towel.

After a couple of days Rosie received help from one of her nieces, who had recovered from the disease. The next day Sidney, our chief assistant, who had been in Brooklyn with his sick brother, showed up and began helping out. Dr. Nash was able to come in every day, and it was with a sense of pride that we began to see our patients start on the road to recovery.

Due to the epidemic, all the banquets and *simchas* (celebrations) had been canceled by the people who had booked them, so there was nothing on our minds except getting everyone in the house back to health. Soon Mother was up, then Frances. Mrs. Goetz's doctor was able to find a nurse, a freshly starched Miss Partridge, who snubbed all of us. She had to be served like a guest. Sidney put up with it because, he said, Miss Partridge was a good-looking chicken. Some months later I heard him talking about this to my father in mysterious and ribald terms; he said that he had had a piece of chicken, a remark I did not fathom at the time.

John was next on his feet, quickly followed by Bubeh, Zaida and Aunt Anna. The last patient was Pa, who finally made it. The newspapers were full of the awful reckoning of the epidemic, and we were grateful that everybody had come through. There were stories that the victims of the sickness were prone to Bright's disease, a cardiac condition and tuberculosis, and we all prayed that no one would suffer these aftereffects.

But the Armistice, on November 11, seemed to clear away the epidemic as well as the war. With the diminution of the epidemic, our business resumed its normal course. I started high school, Lil began rehearsals for the new "Y" show, and life settled down to its regular routine of work.

One night, after a wedding, we were all sitting in the kitchen, eating and talking about the affair we had just catered. When Mother told us that the bride's family had lost a child in the epidemic, the conversation turned to anecdotes about the siege in our house. Lil related that one night she had stopped Pa from his horrendous snoring only by yelling "Shut up" at him. Pa laughed and said it was a good thing he hadn't heard; he'd have gotten up and slapped her face.

But Lil and I received many compliments from everyone, and Mother said something that is considered by Jewish families as the most generous thing a parent can say to a child. She mentioned the endless alcohol rubs we had given, and said, "*Kinder,* you have *goldeneh hent*" (Children, you have golden hands).

I don't think I fully appreciated the compliment, but Lillian did; she broke into tears and sobs, and we all tried to comfort her. Finally Frances made her laugh by giving a perfect imitation of the snooty Miss Partridge.

8

I Lose the Name "Shrimp"

Perhaps if Pa had been psychoanalyzed it might have been discovered that he disliked short men because they reminded him of his father. Whatever the reason, the fact was that he was always suspicious of little men; he maintained that they were arrogant and were always trying to prove themselves. When he did make friends with a short man he viewed him as an exception that proved his rule. He would say of Louis Hare, a man he respected and liked, the chief executive of the Christian Schmidt furniture store, where Pa had worked as a window dresser, "He's a wonderful person even though he's a shrimp."

Pa's initial disappointment in me was because I was short. He often called me "Shrimp." I was afraid of Pa because he dominated our house with a strong hand and an authoritative voice, but I also admired him because he was so big, so strong and so impressive. It was comforting to hear people say, "He's Hugo Schary's son," and I used to hope that I would grow as tall and strong as my father so that he would be pleased with me.

But on my thirteenth birthday I was still only five feet five. It was depressing; since I was now at the bar mitzvah age and taking the obligations of manhood, it seemed to me that I should be assuming a man's stature.

As I have related earlier, in the fall of 1918 I was beat up on Yom Kippur by some Newark youngsters, and I had barely recovered from that embarrassment when I was the first one to catch *The Spanish Influenza.* When all of the family had recovered from that epidemic, my father bought me a bicycle. (He had been told that the stretching of muscles while pushing the pedals was stimulating to growth.) But Pa had misgivings about the traffic, and he urged me to be careful of "the damn machines," which were becoming more numerous on High Street.

The bike was a beautiful red Harley-Davidson with a coaster brake, and I rode it on errands and on visits to some of my old friends on Thirteenth Avenue. It had a basket set in front of the handle bars, and when I rode up to Wigler's bakery or Buchacher's grocery store to collect supplies, I felt like a Pony Express rider taking on a saddlebag of mail.

Buchacher's grocery was owned by Mr. and Mrs. Samuel Buchacher, two handsome Russian Jews, who had four beautiful daughters: Mary, Esther, Frieda and Molly. Though all the girls were older than I, it was my hope that one of them would wait around for me to catch up with her. The store was a magical place. Tubs of butter, barrels of pickles and herrings, bins of coffee, stacks of bread, slabs of lox and mounds of cheese sent out an aroma that always sparked my appetite, and before I would set out for the long journey home (ten blocks seemed like ten miles if you were riding through hostile Indian territory), Mr. Buchacher, who had hair like snow and cheeks like apples, would make me a sandwich of cheese and lox on a roll to sustain me.

In November of 1919 I was whizzing down High Street a short distance from Schary Manor. Approaching Court Street, I was aware of a coal truck on my left. As we both came near the turn down Court Street Hill, I realized that the truck intended to turn right to head down the hill. I decided to try and race ahead and in front of him before he completed the turn. I didn't make it. I hit the side of the truck. The driver had swerved to avoid hitting me, and as I fell I landed between the front and back wheels. I remember hearing the tinkling of my red bike as it smashed on the street; in a daze I became aware that I was lying on the pavement with the left side of my body jammed against the right back wheel of the truck. I had been dragged for a few feet, but at the time I didn't know that.

I didn't feel anything except a dreadful embarrassment—I had wet my pants. Hands dragged me off the street onto the pavement, and then the truck driver and his assistant left me and rolled down the hill and out of my life. I didn't think I was dying, but I knew that I'd never be able to get up and walk. A passer-by came over and talked to me; I heard someone else say there was no name on the coal truck. Then I saw a friendly face; it belonged to Scotty, the Negro janitor of the First Presbyterian Church, which was on the corner of High and Court streets. He bent down and asked me how I felt and told me not to worry, he was going to get my father. He asked someone to watch over me while he went to the Manor.

Just as he hurried off around the corner, Dr. Sam Hirschberg, who lived a block away from us, came by in his automobile. He stopped, took a look, lifted me into his car, and drove me to his office for quick repairs. The other passers-by moved on. In the meanwhile Scotty had gone to Schary Manor and had learned from Rosie Carter that my father wasn't home. He asked for Mother, and in an effort to ease the blow began, "Now, Mrs. Schary, don't be frightened, he ain't dead."

Petrified when she learned what had happened, Mother ran out of the house, followed by my sister Lillian. At the scene of the accident there was nothing left except the wreckage of the bike; Mother later told me that it was the scariest sight of her life. One passer-by told her that a doctor had come and whisked me away, but he didn't know where.

Mother and Lil ran back to the house and to the telephone. The first hospital they called was the Beth Israel, but they had no record of a young Schary. Lil called St. Barnabas' and St. Vincent's. Then Father arrived home and took over. He called a friend of his, Detective Lipsky, who arrived quickly from the First Precinct. A mounting terror began to grow in Mother, Father, Lil and Detective Lipsky. They each had one thought—the city morgue—but each was afraid to suggest it.

In Dr. Hirschberg's office, only a block and a half

away, I was being washed, medicated and bandaged. The left side of my torso from hip to shoulder had been bruised and lacerated. My left thigh had been hurt and my shoulder scraped, but the only mark on my face was a slight cut on my forehead. Dr. Hirschberg and his nurse did a fine job, even though his specialty was ear, nose and throat. After they had finished they called my mother.

Mother, Father, Lil and Detective Lipsky got to the doctor's office a few minutes later. In an effort to relieve their anxiety, I insisted on standing up to greet them. But I couldn't walk. Father lifted me into his arms and carried me home, with the rest of them, including Dr. Hirschberg, trailing along. They put me to bed and Dr. Hirschberg gave me some elixir of luminal. For days I was nursed and coddled. I didn't mind a bit. Father sat with me and said that shrimp or no shrimp, he'd never let me ride a bicycle again. Each night he brought me a gift—a book or some candy or a new necktie or sweater.

After ten days, just as I was feeling better and stronger, I came down with a bad sore throat. It was the first sign of diphtheria. Dr. Nash arrived with Dr. Hirschberg and gave me a shot of serum, but for many days I was quite ill. I would lie in bed and listen to the sounds of the parties going on downstairs. The orchestra played all my favorite songs, and I thought of all the money I was losing on the hat-check concession. (Later Lil generously donated my one-third take to me, despite the fact that I had been unable to work.)

At night Frances came in and read to me from *Huckleberry Finn* and *The Last of the Mohicans*. As a result I went on to read all of Twain and Cooper. She told me to dream of getting well and to dream of doing what I wanted to do; dreams are what make life worth living, she said. So I dreamed. I began to dream of being a writer. One day Frances brought me a new pad and some pencils and told me to dream on paper. I wrote a war story about American soldiers escaping from the terrible Boches.

Some time later I was able to sit up, and soon I was allowed to get out of bed. But the first day up, I began to feel pain in my throat again. Drs. Nash and Hirschberg showed up in tandem and diagnosed this latest discomfort as tonsillitis. Dr. Hirschberg said that the tonsils had to go, and Dr. Nash agreed. As soon as the acute infection subsided, Dr. Hirschberg brought over his gear and he and Dr. Nash performed the tonsillectomy in the bedroom on a table brought up from the banquet room. I felt like a meal that was about to be served.

The operation put me back in bed for another long spell, because by now I was tired and my resistance was low. Pa worried about me; he came in every day and told me to be strong. He told me stories of his youth and sang songs to me and promised that when I was well we would go to Lakewood for a long vacation.

During this siege I began to devour books: all the Boy Allies and Tom Swift series, the Leatherstocking Tales, *Oliver Twist*, tales of Texas by Altsheler, the Zane Grey books, and all of the Tarzan stories. For the first time I began to feel the pride of possession in owning books.

Eventually my throat healed, and after the long spell I was eager to get up and get out. But I wasn't quite ready for that; the second day after I began to wander about the bedroom, I got a severe pain in my stomach. This time Dr. Nash came with Dr. Danzis, and they prodded, palpated and pushed my belly. Dr. Danzis said it was acute appendicitis, and an hour later I was in the Beth Israel Hospital. Pa and Ma looked ashen with worry, but they tried to reassure me by saying that the operation was not a difficult one. Bubeh was with them, and she put her hands on my head and assured me I was going to be all right. She told me to keep my hands clenched tightly—it would help keep me strong. I had some doubts, but I obeyed her instruction. The next thing I knew, I was alive and minus my appendix.

Once again my recovery was slow. I'd had a long siege of illness and lost a lot of weight and the doctors said I must spend many weeks in bed. I didn't mind; I felt exhausted.

When I finally was well again, November, December, January, February and March had gone by. To everyone's astonishment, I had grown four and one-half inches while in bed. None of my clothes fitted.

Father was absolutely delighted. When I was able to go out, he took me to Weber and Heilbroner's and bought me a brand new wardrobe. When I tried something on that was too small, he beamed with pride. "It's too small," he'd say. "Get him a man's size. He's no shrimp."

As Pa had promised, we went to Lakewood for a short holiday. Then my brother Sam asked me to spend the summer with him and his wife, Elsie. It was a magnificent summer, and when I got back I was fourteen years old, almost six feet tall, thin as a pencil, and ready for my long-pants wardrobe, which Pa bought me with pleasure and extravagance.

Forever after Pa always called me "Son" with added affection. And perhaps because I felt I had provided him with some fulfillment, I loved him more than I had before.

Dr. Nash never could understand what had happened, but he cheerfully accepted the fact that before I had been run over I had to stand on my toes to let him look at my throat, while afterward he had to stand on *his* toes to peek inside.

9

The Ten-Dollar Menu with Flowers, Please

It was raining and I was in the office of Schary Manor reading a book by Zane Grey. Lillian was talking on the telephone to a friend about the new show at the Y.M.H.A.; she was going to sing one of the leading roles, and her part, that of a famous star, got bigger and better as she talked about it. When the doorbell rang Lillian, in the haughty tones of a leading lady, gave me a peremptory order to answer it. But Zane Grey's story had cast me into the role of a cowhand. So I gave my sister a long hard look, my blue eyes squinting with restrained and righteous anger and my right hand held clawlike for a quick draw.

The doorbell rang again. "Will you please answer-r-r?" The word "answer" was stretched to project impatience, contempt, weariness and command. It is a sound that can only be made by an eighteen-year-old sister speaking to a fourteen-year-old brother.

I slouched to the door, my legs bowed from years in the saddle. As I opened it I was ready for rustler, Indian or arrogant sheriff. But standing in the hallway was a young woman, wearing a cloche hat and a wet overcoat, drying her face with a handkerchief. She smiled at me and asked if Mrs. Schary was home. I directed her to the office, then went to the kitchen to call my mother, who was making a strudel.

"A lady wants to see you, Ma."

"I'll be there in a minute."

I nodded and watched as Mother stretched the strudel dough. This procedure always fascinated me. Mother was a marvelous cook and much of the marvel was in watching her work. The white cloth sprinkled with flour was covered by the dough, stretched paper-thin, and Mother's hands kept working under the dough, coaxing it and cajoling it. A thick spot was attacked and soon disappeared; a bubble was gently smoothed without bursting. The dough was pulled and manipulated from paper thinness to tissue thinness. Then Mother sprinkled oil to keep it moist, then the crushed apples, cinnamon, raisins, sugar and finely chopped nuts. The sprinkling had to be perfectly even, and finally the strudel was rolled. To me this was always the suspenseful part: Would it run from the cloth, spin away from Mother's careful urging, and plunge to the floor?

At the fateful moment Mother looked up, surprised that I was still in the kitchen, and said, "Sonny, that's not very nice. Tell the lady I'll be with her in a minute. Go on now."

I hurried out, but took one last look. Mother was handling the rolling as well as always, with just the tip of her tongue visible at the corner of her mouth to reveal her own suspense.

When I got to the office, Lillian was hanging up the telephone. The lady had taken off her coat, and now she and Lillian exchanged a nod.

"I'm Lillian Schary, Mrs. Schary's younger daughter."

"My name is Thelma Weiss. My father is Samuel Weiss, the glazier."

It was a normal greeting. In the Jewish community of Newark it was habitual to identify yourself through your parents.

"This is my kid brother," Lillian said by way of introducing me.

"I have already had the pleasure of his acquaintance." Miss Weiss smiled at me and immediately I was her slave. Just then Mother entered the office, flicking back the strand of hair that was always falling over her forehead, her face flushed as it always was when she came from work in the kitchen.

"Hello," said Miss Weiss, "I'm Thelma Weiss. I'm the daughter of Samuel Weiss, the glazier."

"Oh, I know your father—and your mother. She works with us at the Home for the Aged. How are your dear parents?"

"Thank you," Miss Weiss said, both as an acknowledgment of appreciation for the inquiry and an assurance that her parents were well. "I'm getting married."

"*Mazeltov*," said Mother. "Who's the lucky groom?"

"You wouldn't know him. He's from out of town. New York State. Rochester. A lawyer. He was in the war."

"That's wonderful," said Mother. "Wonderful."

"So I'd like to arrange for the wedding."

Immediately Lillian went to the desk for the date book and some blank contracts and I put down Zane Grey. I was sorry that Miss Weiss was marrying that lawyer from Rochester; I wished she was marrying me. She had a sweet look in her eyes and beautiful white teeth, and I knew that I was madly in love with her.

Mother asked Miss Weiss why her parents hadn't come along. She explained that her father was very busy and her mother had rheumatism and didn't like to travel in rainy weather, and anyway she wanted to have the fun of arranging things by herself. "After all," she laughed, "it's my first wedding."

Mother laughed as if she hadn't heard it said by a thousand brides-to-be. I smiled at Miss Weiss; I wanted her to know I appreciated everything she said. Lillian paid no attention; she was placing carbon paper between copies of the contract blanks and I could see that now she was playing the role of the efficient businesswoman.

"Well," said Mother, "then let's get down to business. What date is the wedding?"

"I'd like June the sixth."

Lillian flicked the pages of the book, then looked up in surprise. "That's a Friday." No Jewish girl was ever married on a Friday; it was the Sabbath.

"Maybe Miss Weiss means the seventh. That's a Saturday."

"Yes, the seventh of June. I want to be a June bride."

"On the seventh, Mother, is the Rosenberg-Fielder wedding. Two hundred couples."

I was annoyed at Lillian, and hated the Rosenbergs and Fielders for being an obstacle to Miss Weiss.

But Miss Weiss was reasonable. "What about the fourteenth of June?"

The fourteenth of June was free. Everyone seemed relieved.

"What menu would you like?" Mother asked.

Miss Weiss asked for a range of the prices and menus.

"Well, dear," Mother said, "we begin with a four-dollar menu—a couple, that is. There's grapefruit with maraschino cherry, gefilte fish or whitefish with lemon sauce, chicken roasted with stuffing, peas, carrots, browned potatoes, hearts of lettuce, strudel, coffee and mints. And you furnish the flowers. We print the menus, like a souvenir, for everybody."

"That sounds very nice, but what's your fanciest menu?"

"That's the ten-dollar-per-couple menu. Very elegant. Fresh pineapple cocktail served in pineapple shells, then gefilte fish or whitefish, chicken soup with noodles or matzoh balls, tongue with sweet and sour sauce, then sherbet, any flavor. Roast chicken, or duck, or stuffed squab, with vegetables served in potato rame-kins, then romaine lettuce with French dressing. For dessert, strudel and ices. Demitasse. Mints. Cigars served at the table. And of course a sweet table before the supper with hors d'oeuvres and nuts and honey cake. We also furnish the flowers and the menus."

"That sounds like heaven," said Miss Weiss. "Like heaven. That's what I want. The ten-dollar menu with flowers, please. Thank you so much." She stood up.

"But, dear," Mother said, "there are other things to talk about."

"Oh," said my lovely Miss Weiss. "What other things?"

Mother explained. "How many couples do you expect? Do you want us to take care of the music?"

"Of course, the music," said Miss Weiss as she sat down. "What's the best?"

"There are many different orchestras. The Glicksteins, the Pashkows, Ralph Reichenthal. You can have four pieces, or six, or eight—even ten."

"I'd like ten. Any orchestra you say."

"Should we serve them?"

"Yes. I want them to be like guests."

There was a pause, then Mother nodded with that little smile which I knew meant she had a secret. She became a trifle more businesslike. "Lillian, make up the contract." Then she turned to Miss Weiss. "You can go, Thelma. Give my best wishes to your darling mother. Tell her *mazeltov*. We will send the contracts to her and she can sign them and send us the deposit."

"The deposit?"

"Yes, dear. We always ask a small deposit to hold the date."

"How much?"

"A hundred dollars. Your father can send a check. No rush."

"Oh, no, oh . . . no," Miss Weiss said. "I want to make the deposit. Please, I must." She opened her purse and dropped some change on the desk along with a crumpled five-dollar bill. Suddenly the rain was harder outside the window, and it had gotten much darker. I was uncomfortable.

Mother looked at the money and then at Miss Weiss. "It isn't necessary, dear."

"I insist. Please."

"Lillian," Mother said, "make out a receipt for a five-dollar deposit."

"No," said Miss Weiss, "there's more. I only need a nickel for the jitney. Here—it's five dollars and sixty-two cents."

"All right, dear. Lillian, make out the receipt." Mother helped Miss Weiss on with her coat and congratulated her once again on her good fortune.

"He's a marvelous man. Wait till you see him, Mrs. Schary." She took the receipt from Lillian and said goodbye to both of us.

Mother escorted Miss Weiss to the door. As she left, Lillian looked at me and twirled a finger near her temple.

"She is not," I said.

The front door closed. Mother returned to the office and told Lillian to look up the telephone number of Samuel Weiss, the glazier on Bergen Street.

"Lillian says she's crazy," I volunteered.

"She is," said Lillian.

Mother said, "Who's to say who's crazy? Get me the number."

Lillian got Mrs. Weiss's number and Mother took the telephone. "Hello, Ruth, darling, how are you? Fine? I'm glad. Your beautiful daughter, Thelma, just left here— Yes, a minute ago. . . . Yes, she arranged for the wedding. . . . I know, darling, I know. Believe me, I'm sorry. . . . No, she was sweet and quiet. . . . I know. It's so very sad. Listen, don't tell Samuel, it will only aggravate him. . . . Believe me, Ruth, no one will tell. . . ." She gave Lillian and me a level look and we both nodded. Suddenly tears came to her eyes. "I know, Ruthie. Maybe in a quiet way somehow you could get some help—you know, from Dr. Nash or somebody. I'll send you back the little money she left. . . . Ruthie, for us it was no trouble. If she comes again, I'll make out like it never happened before. . . . Ruthie, darling, listen to me, don't be ashamed. . . . God bless you. Goodbye." Mother hung up, reached for her handkerchief, blew her nose and wiped her eyes, then shook her head. "It's a curse, a curse," she said.

"You knew about it, Mother?" Lillian asked.

"Yes. Mrs. Weiss told me about her daughter. It's so sad. The poor girl has . . . daydreams. So she arranges for her wedding. She goes to the hotels, to Kalisch's, and finally she came here. Her mother told me weeks ago that she might."

"Holy mackerel," I said, "she is crazy, isn't she, Ma?"

Mother shrugged. "I don't know what crazy is. Like I say, she dreams. Look, don't you dream? You want to be a writer, an actor, a soldier? Lillian dreams, too—she wants to be a great singer."

"Yes, Mother," said Lillian, "but this is different!"

"How so much different? We all make believe a little. This girl doesn't hurt anybody. All she cost us was a little time and two pieces of paper. Tear it up and send the money to Mrs. Weiss."

"Mother, that girl ought to be in an institution," Lillian said.

"Who should send her," said Ma, "her mother?" She walked out of the office.

10

The Happy Ramblers

Occasionally the orthodox Jewish population that was clustered around Prince Street in Newark would have a parade. These processions, in celebration of a Jewish festival or in honor of the dedication of a new Hebrew school or synagogue, seldom included more than two or three hundred people. The marchers usually took the same route, a square bordered by Prince, Kinney, High and Court streets. A small band always preceded the marchers and most of the songs were gay Jewish ones, interspersed with American marches. It was incongruous, but lovely, to see bearded elderly Jews striding along to "The Stars and Stripes Forever."

These parades never attracted as much attention as

the military or circus parades. They were small and had little color; they lacked the sparkling uniforms or handsome Indians on horseback and glorious whistling music of the calliope. But always there were some spectators who were drawn by curiosity or by relationship to one of the marchers. As the men marched, carefully avoiding the souvenirs left by horses, they would wave and call out, "Hello," "*Mazeltov*," "*Vus machst du?*" (How are you?) or "*Kuk unds un*" (Look us over). In turn, the spectators would be shouting, "Hello, Moishe," "Hey, Maxie," "*Mazeltov*, Reb Brodsky."

But always there were the tormentors, usually tough, hard-muscled young Poles. The heart of the opposition was in Wickliffe Street, and when the Jews celebrated, the Poles would venture out looking for sport.

In Newark, gang war was not uncommon, but happily it lacked the intensity of modern-day neighborhood warfare with its switch blades, zip guns, chains and marijuana. The Irish had a strong contingent of warriors; so did the Italians, who were mostly located in the "down neck" section of town. But the Irish and Jewish districts breathed next to each other, so Jewish holidays and St. Patrick's Days were inevitable times for conflict. Sometimes on Columbus Day the Irish and Jews would join together and go prowling for trouble in the Italian quarter.

Most of the time there was little friction. We all had friends in enemy camps, and these friendships would thrive and not even be affected by the battles that took place during holidays or at the end of a heavy snowfall. It was the custom then to build a solid fort and stock it with snowballs, iced by dipping them in pails of cold water. Then we would wait to be stormed by the invaders. After a brisk fight, it was expected that we would pay a return visit and try to destroy our attackers' fort. Usually the day ended with both forts leveled, everybody soaked with snow, and a few of us decorated with shiners as a result of lucky hits.

But this rivalry on the part of the Jews, sometimes painful but also having some degree of camaraderie, existed only with the Irish, the Italians, and some of the Negroes. It never existed with the Poles, who had brought over from Europe their active hostility toward the Jews, who, in turn, responded with their old-world fear of the Poles. Most of the Jews had fled pogroms in Russia and Poland. In America they had a fighting chance against the Poles—and they took it. Gang fights were brutal, tough and far beyond the fiber and skill of young kids; the older teen-agers and youths in their twenties reserved these brannigans for themselves.

Therefore when the Jews had a parade, it was almost certain that they would be molested by trouble-hunting Poles, who would yell obscenities and try to provoke active combat. They would run up to some of the older men, yank at their beards and try to knock off their hats, knowing that this indignity would be particularly embarrassing to orthodox Jews, who never uncovered their heads. It was considered good fun. The older Jews would yell back obscenities in Polish, which most of them spoke, or in Yiddish, and sometimes in rugged and explicit English.

But the Happy Ramblers were not content with verbal retaliation. While no one knew how the Happy Ramblers came into existence—it was known why. Organized to defend the religious community from incursions by hostile neighbors, they were an unofficial Haganah, and their headquarters was the large office of the Amsterdam Moving Company, where many of them worked as truck drivers or movers. Other members of the gang included taxi drivers, "prelim" prizefighters, basketball players and young college students who spent their free time at Amsterdam's, playing pool, playing cards or chess, shooting the breeze or ogling the pretty girls. They came and went, depending on working or school hours, or how they made out with the girls; whichever, there were always a large enough group of Ramblers hanging around to answer a call for help. They would pile into one of the Amsterdam trucks, roll to the scene of action, and deploy for battle. In a troubled area there was always one Jew who knew about the Happy Ramblers and how to reach them.

John, our Polish janitor, liked our family, and we liked him. It was a kind of reverse snobbery. We thought of him as "an acceptable Pole" in the same way some people think of "an acceptable Jew."

John proved his loyalties to us one autumn day in 1919 when there was a parade to welcome a new synagogue opening up on Morton Street. Zaida was marching. He liked parades; he had served as a soldier in the Czar's army, and though he no longer played the tuba, he still had a good ear for a brass band. Of course we waited outside Schary Manor for the procession to come by before it moved up Court Street. When John heard the music, he came up from the pantry, and as the procession came toward us he proclaimed his joy with his single English word, "Sonamonbitch."

But trouble was also coming our way. Polish hoodlums were already thronging the streets, and pushing and yelling could be seen and heard even three blocks away. Then an Amsterdam truck glided to a stop near us and from the back of it some fourteen or fifteen husky young men descended and headed in the direction of the parade. The Happy Ramblers had been sent for to halt the depredations of the attacking Poles from Wickliffe Street.

The Ramblers' technique was always the same. They would join the spectators, and when an overt act of aggression occurred they would tap the transgressor on the shoulder and ask pleasantly, "Russki Polski?" If the answer was yes (delivered either in English or Polish), a Jewish fist exploded in the transgressor's face.

There were seldom more than one or two fighters in any one place at one time; the enemy was usually spread out, and so were the defenders. A policeman on horseback might be patrolling the vicinity, but by the time he rode up to investigate one fight, another would be taking place somewhere else. Sometimes a figure would remain lying on the pavement, but usually at the end of a scuffle someone would be running with a broken nose or torn lip or split eye.

Of course there were casualties among the Ramblers too, because as their strength increased so did the strength of the Poles, who also had prize fighters, piano movers and weight lifters in their section of town.

On this occasion we saw some action as the parade moved toward us. Soon we spotted Zaida swinging along in step with the band. He was wearing a straight-brimmed straw hat and his beard was pointed almost straight out in front of him as he held his head high. Suddenly a young man moved into the line of march and started to berate some of the walkers. As he approached Zaida, John moved off the porch, saying something in Polish which I didn't understand. With weak faith, I thought that this was the hour of betrayal; John was leaving to join his friends.

I misjudged his intent. John moved up to the young fellow, who was about to put his hand on Zaida's beard. Spinning the tormentor around, he struck him in the belly with both hands clenched together in one mighty fist. Then another young Pole jumped in and belted John. Zaida, still marching in step, hit the newcomer over the head with his cane, but the blow did no damage compared to the wallop John now delivered to this second intruder. By this time two of the Happy Ramblers had come up and I was on my way toward Zaida. Bubeh and Mother were on the porch, moaning in excitement, and a mounted policeman was galloping toward the disturbance. Though they had come to a halt to witness the scuffle, the members of the band were still playing a merry Jewish tune. Some of the musicians lost interest in their playing, however, and the volume of music decreased in an odd, unresolved series of musical phrases.

By now John was confused but no less eager to protect Zaida. When one of the Ramblers arrived, John belted him for good measure. The other Rambler, assuming that he was one of the enemy, assaulted John. Now Zaida hit this Rambler on the head with his cane and yelled at him in Yiddish. Another Pole rushed in and John slugged *him*. This added to the puzzlement of the two Ramblers who, quite understandably, didn't know whose side John was on.

Luckily Zaida's Yiddish was effective and he

straightened matters out. John had been hit in the eye, which was swelling rapidly. Zaida took him by the arm and left the parade. Pursued with additional punches and kicks, the Poles hurriedly left the battleground; the band, encouraged by the Irish policeman who called in Yiddish, *"Lummir gehen"* (Let's go), started playing again. Off the procession went, followed by the rest of the marchers—all now well protected by the Happy Ramblers, who had routed the rest of the raiders.

By the time we got John back to the Manor, his eye was almost shut. Mother sat him down and put a large piece of beef on his bruised cheek. In various tones of anger, annoyance and surprise, John kept repeating, "Sonamonbitch." Zaida and Mother talked to him in Polish. Of course they were grateful to him, and Zaida jokingly suggested that they ought to make John an honorary member of the B'nai B'rith. When Father came home that afternoon, he heard the story and was grieved that he hadn't been there to join in the fight. He too was grateful to John and treated him to a large glass of schnapps.

From that time on, John was recognized by the Happy Ramblers as an ally and friend whenever he went to Prince Street with Mother to shop for chickens or fish. How he was viewed by his Polish neighbors, I don't know. He lived in our house in a room in the basement, and I don't remember that he ever went back to Wickliffe Street where his Polish friends lived.

11

The Case of the Crying Bridegroom

The Finkels were in the coal business. There was Mr. Finkel and Mrs. Finkel and five sons named Abraham, Benjamin, David, Daniel and Irving. They were Russian Jews, and en masse they were the biggest family I ever saw. They were all black-haired, ruddy-cheeked, and had deep brown eyes; they were broad, their heads were set into their shoulders with no necks in between, and they had huge hands and big feet. On holidays in temple the six Finkel males sat cramped in a pew built for eight people of average size; they seemed to be spilling out of it. When they rose and sat down together during the services, they gave the illusion of a sliding wall that went up and down.

As the boys finished grade school they moved into

their father's business. They had all grown strong lifting baskets of coal, driving the big trucks and shoveling tons of anthracite. All together the family was as impressive as the Alleghenies.

The Finkels had fared well in business, and it was a happy day when the oldest son, Abraham, was engaged to be married. His bride was from a good Jewish family. Though her parents weren't rich, her father was a respected Talmudist, who earned his living as a Hebrew teacher. Her mother was a midwife. We heard that the marriage had been arranged by a *shadchen,* a marriage broker, who acts as the agent for the Lord. Many Orthodox Jews believe that all marriages are arranged in heaven, and the *shadchen* claims to be able to figure out who belongs, by predestination, to whom.

Despite the fact that Abraham's bride-to-be was not going to bring much of a dowry with her, the Finkels were satisfied that it was a good match. She was a pretty girl who had graduated from high school and normal school and was now teaching arithmetic to sixth graders. Both the Finkels and the bride's parents, the Rosens, came to arrange for the wedding. The Finkels knew that the Rosens couldn't afford an expensive affair, but since Abraham was the first of the Finkels to be pledged, they wanted to chip in and make the wedding a gala one.

The four parents picked a date in June. The menu was to be eight dollars a couple, and they asked us to book Jerry Norton's orchestra and gave us authority to spend three hundred dollars for flowers and decorations.

Abraham and his bride-to-be, Evelyn, gleamed with happiness. Everything was fine—except Grandma Finkel's health. She was a lady in her eighty-ninth year and as black, strong and big as the Finkels, but she had become ill a few weeks before the wedding. All the Finkels prayed for her to stay alive so that she could have the joy of being present at the marriage of her oldest grandson, but the prayers went unheard and the old matriarch passed away with loud and violent lamentations from the Finkel family. She was thoughtful enough to depart far enough ahead, so that the mourning period did not interfere with the wedding.

Nevertheless the Finkels were a stunned and still-grieving family as they prepared for the wedding night. There were one hundred and fifty guests. The affair was formal; this meant that for weeks Jewish men had been arranging to rent tuxedos and full-dress suits from Louis Lesser (the most successful outfitter in Newark; his slogan was "Louis Lesser, the Full Dresser, Upstairs, sir. Yes, Sir!"). Few families in Newark had their own formal suits. Louis Lesser had laid in a large supply of suits and accessories; as the catering business boomed, so did Louis Lesser (no relation to Louis *Lasser*, who sold men's suits but didn't rent them).

All the guests who trooped in on the night of the wedding were handsomely dressed. But they were also aware of the recent loss in the Finkel family and wore appropriately solemn expressions.

Before the ceremony there were drinks and cookies at the "sweet table," and then the guests sat down to wait for the event to get under way. The Finkels arrived in a rented sedan that groaned under their weight. Even Louis Lesser had not been equal to the task of outfitting the Finkel men. They bulged out of their full-dress suits; their starched white shirt fronts kept ballooning out of their vests; they craned their heads to relieve themselves of the pressure exerted by their wing collars; high hats perched precariously on their heads. The Finkel men were a magnificent sight.

Mama Finkel was dressed in an elegant black lace dress covered with sequins. There were many sequins because there was so much of Mama Finkel. The dress had been tailored for her—it had to be. The family all retired to the second floor to wait for the ceremony. They were all thinking about poor Grandma Finkel, who wouldn't be there on this festive evening.

As a matter of fact the Finkels seemed to be doing their best to make it less festive. The bridegroom, in particular, was deeply bereaved. His grandmother had loved him and he had loved her. When he was little she had taught him many songs and games. (Lil irreverently suggested that she had probably taught him how to carry a basket of coal.)

Now Evelyn Rosen, the bride, arrived with her mother and father. The marriage broker was downstairs greeting some of his friends and keeping an eye open for possible future alliances. My father was already looking at his watch, a sign that he was becoming impatient. The orchestra was in place and Jerry Norton was leading them in the playing of such standards as "Kiss Me Again," "I Love You Truly" and "Roses of Picardy." Rabbi Brodsky arrived a bit late, but after a short schnapps downstairs with Zaida he was ready. He put on his robes, his *talis,* and his large puffed-out rabbi's cap, and took his position beneath the red-velvet *chupah,* which was supported by long brass rods set into holes in the floor. The *chazan,* the cantor, stood to one side, ready to intone the ritualistic singing prayers.

Lil was going to sing "Oh, Promise Me" to start

the ceremony, so I had checked most of the guests'
coats while she was upstairs changing into her formal
dress. Pa was roaming around the hall, urging people
to sit down and get ready for "the cermony" (he never
said "ceremony," always "cermony"). We were running
a normal forty minutes behind schedule, but soon everything was ready. The bridal party was lined up in place
by Frances; the guests were seated; Lil was modestly
secreted behind some palms; and on instructions from
Pa I waved to Jerry, and the orchestra started to play.

Lil came in right on cue and sang "Oh, Promise
Me" in her sweet contralto and Jerry swung into the
wedding march. The guests turned to watch the procession. The three ushers, David, Daniel and Irving Finkel,
brought Pa Finkel down the aisle. They all looked sad
and on the verge of tears. Then came Mrs. Rosen, supported by her son Morris. They all stood around the
canopy until finally the groom arrived, accompanied by
his mother, the two of them a moving mountain of
gloom as they approached. Next there appeared the
maid of honor; as she came into view the orchestra
played Wagner's "Wedding March" from *Lohengrin*.

Lastly there was Evelyn, escorted by her father.
They seemed to be the only two people participating
in a wedding; Mr. Rosen was beaming and Evelyn was
radiant. But her appearance brought no smiles from the
bridegroom and his family; Evelyn only seemed to remind them of the fact that Grandma Finkel wasn't there
to share their happiness.

When all were in place and the music had faded
away, Rabbi Brodsky began on a thoughtful, but un-
fortunate, note. "When we gather for a happy occasion,

we think back to those loved ones who are not able to be with us . . ."

He got no further. The bridegroom broke into muffled sobbing; so did his father, mother, brothers, and all his relatives grouped before the canopy.

The sound surprised Rabbi Brodsky; he stopped in astonishment. Pa was outraged and attempted to halt the tide of bereavement. It was a valiant but useless effort; by now the bridegroom, Abraham, was sobbing, "I want my Grandma." Pa was a determined man, however; he strode down the aisle and whispered, "Ssssh, sssh, quiet, the cermony is going on."

Suddenly Mr. Finkel's sister, a daughter of the departed, called loudly, *"Ich halish"* (I'm fainting). It is an interesting coincidence that all elderly Jewish women rise and announce their coming state of unconsciousness as a sort of warning to everyone to be prepared. As Pa Finkel's sister rose to her feet with her cry of distress, there was the expected murmur of excitement, after which she proceeded to faint.

By this time my father had completely lost control of himself and of the situation and was running up and down the aisle calling plaintively "What's the matter with all of you? This is a happy occasion! It's a wedding! Laugh—ha! ha!—laugh!"

But no one laughed, and when Sister Finkel fell to the floor, other ladies announced that they were about to faint. Father rushed to Miss Finkel—who was roughly the same size, color and weight as the rest of her family—bent down, scooped her up, and straining beneath the enormity of his task, carried her out and up one flight of steps to the bride's dressing room. After him came two doctors from the congregation, Lil, Frances and I.

Sister Finkel was quickly revived, and Father told us to go downstairs and see that the "cermony" went on. When we got there, order had been restored. Furious at the interruption, Rabbi Brodsky had abandoned his English and was telling the participants and the guests what he thought of them in eloquent and scalding Yiddish. He told them to be quiet or he'd leave the house. His words of reprimand restored propriety and the interrupted ceremony was begun again.

This time all went well. At the conclusion Abraham stepped on the glass to break it, thus reminding everyone of the destruction of the Temple and marking an end to the ceremony, and the band struck up Mendelssohn's "Wedding March" known to everyone as "Gee Whiz, I'm Glad I'm Free." There was no formal receiving line; the guests merely swarmed forward and kissed the bride and groom, called out *"Mazeltov,"* kissed each other and laughed and cried happy tears.

A wedding is always a happy time in Jewish life, partly because it is related to the happiness and peace of the Sabbath, the day that is considered to be the Bride of the Week. So once Rabbi Brodsky had brought everyone to heel, they forgot their initial sorrow and behaved as they were supposed to. Champagne glasses were passed around by the waiters, music was playing, and in a few moments Sister Finkel returned to the party, refreshed and rather pleased with herself at having attracted so much attention.

But I couldn't find Father. Lil didn't know where he was and neither did Frances. When we discovered that he wasn't in the kitchen, we all got worried. Mother led us on a search; Lillian and Frances went downstairs to the pantries and I went upstairs with Mother.

We found Father on his bed. He had a towel over his mouth. I could see bloodstains on it.

He called to Mother, "Get him out of the room. I've got tuberculosis."

Mother sent me out. Tuberculosis was my father's special fear. Three of his brothers had died of the disease and he had been suspected of having it when he was young. Now that he found himself spitting blood, he was convinced that the white plague had caught up with him.

Though I knew something about his phobia at the time, I knew little about tuberculosis; however, I do remember being amazed that the disease could reach out and seize a victim so quickly. At that moment Mother came to the bedroom door and told me to call Dr. Nash and ask him to come over right away. I ran to the office and told Lillian and Frances that Father was dying of tuberculosis. Lillian pushed me away from the phone; she was sure that the operator would get Dr. Nash's number more quickly for her than for me. Frances ran upstairs to Father.

In the meanwhile Mother and Frank and Sidney had gotten the guests seated and the dinner under way. Then Dr. Nash arrived. He was a good-looking man, prematurely gray, and very appealing to me because he had a faint lisp that made him seem friendly and less "doctory." He assured Father that it was practically impossible for anybody to get tuberculosis in twenty minutes. He questioned him closely about the events of the evening, then grinned and called him a damned fool. "First of all," he said, "you must have ruptured a blood vessel when you picked up that horse of a woman. Second, if you're not careful you'll aggravate your hernia."

Pa was sure he hadn't done that; he'd worn a truss for years and it had never failed him. But he stayed in bed for a few days and then went to Atlantic City to "breathe some sea breeze." When he returned he was tanned and well and reassured that he didn't have tuberculosis.

The Finkels lived happily ever after. Benjamin and David and Daniel, by this time resigned to Grandma Finkel's absence, were all married in Schary Manor within the next few years—without tears.

12

Hail the Conquering Hero

Until Uncle Jack returned to the United States in 1919 I don't think I had ever seen him. I had heard stories about him, but they were vague and guarded. He was the younger brother of my mother and Aunt Bessie, but Zaida never mentioned his name. For reasons I never knew, Zaida had rent his garments, said Kaddish (the prayer of affirmation in God's judgment whenever there is a death in a family), and now thought of Uncle Jack only as someone who had died long ago.

I did know that Uncle Jack had run away from home a long time ago, after he had come home from a reform school. Then in 1912 he had written to my Aunt Bessie to tell her that he had enlisted in the Army. He had been with General Pershing during the half-hearted invasion of Mexico to capture Pancho Villa, then had gone off to join the English army and help win World War I for the Allies.

His "departure" from the American Army was kept secret by Uncle Jack, and when he finally wrote to my Aunt Bess he had changed his name and was on his way to Gallipoli. Some old letters of his written from Mesopotamia tell of wounds received in action. His prose was eloquent, and in most of the letters he refers to himself as a sinner who was trying to expiate his past failings in battle. One letter of 1918 tells of his plan to go to India and join up with some English volunteers who were to be sent into battle against the Bolsheviki inside Russia. But illnesses and his wounds kept him out of that adventure. Early in 1919 my mother told me Uncle Jack was coming home.

Uncle Jack's return presented a serious problem. Mother discussed it with Bubeh, who was eager to see her son, but Zaida only repeated what he had often said: "My son is dead, I can't see him."

Mother and Aunt Bessie talked matters over with Rabbi Brodsky, who was kind and understanding but said there was nothing he could do about Zaida's decision. I doubt that he even tried to do anything about it. The Russian Jews who emigrated to America were usually stubborn, sturdy and pious folk; it was almost impossible to get them to reverse their judgments.

I knew little of the background of all this at that time; all I did know was that Uncle Jack had been a hero who had fought at the Dardanelles and that he was coming home weighed down with decorations and glory. His shadowy past was intriguing and romantic to me, my sisters and my cousins, Sam and Belle Pocker, who were Aunt Bess's children.

Finally the family decided that it would be best for Zaida to go away for a few days to my Uncle Meyer's farm in Flemington, New Jersey, during the time of Uncle Jack's visit. I was scheduled to go too, but I managed to beg off. (During my first visit there, some years before, I had run a fishhook through my right thumb and had been laid low by poison ivy. Also, I had become disenchanted with Uncle Meyer; when I was sick at his farm, he had aided my recovery by promising me a pony. He never delivered it, and though I knew that if I had gotten the pony there would have been no place to stable him, I remained unforgiving.)

So Zaida went willingly to Flemington with his brother-in-law, Feter Dudy, and Bubeh stayed home with us. Mother was certain that Zaida knew what was going on, but while he wouldn't see Jack, he didn't want to deprive Bubeh. For all his stubbornness and his orthodoxy, Zaida was exceptionally tolerant of other people's weaknesses. After my bar mitzvah I was supposed to put on *t'filin* each morning. This ceremony consists of winding leather phylacteries around the hands and left arm and placing the box containing the first affirmation of Judaism on the forehead. It is ordered in Deuteronomy: "Hear, O Israel: the Lord our God, the Lord is One. . . . And these words which I command thee this day shall be in thy heart. . . . And thou shalt bind them for a sign upon thine hand, and they shall be for frontlets between thine eyes. And thou shalt write them upon the door posts of thy house and upon thy gates."

But within a few weeks I began to rush through my morning prayers. I would skip most of them and hurry through the rest. Knowing that Zaida would ask me to roll up my sleeve to show him the marks left by the leather thongs, I would pull hard upon the strap to prove I'd recited all my prayers. From the short time it took me to breeze past the prayers, Zaida must have known that I was cheating. I was sure of it one morning when he said to me, "You can recite your prayers faster than a rabbi. You are a true *melamed* [teacher]. I could learn from you."

After a while, by tacit agreement, I stopped reporting to Zaida and he stopped asking me to bare my arm. I know my defection brought him disappointment, but perhaps he would derive some wry satisfaction if he knew that now I am a better student of Hebrew and Judaism than in those days when I tried to deceive him.

The day after Zaida left for Flemington, Jack arrived at Schary Manor with Aunt Bess, who had traveled with him from New York. My first view of him was disappointing. He was short, not tall; he was quite bald, instead of having a shock of black hair swept by the wind of battle; he was slight, rather than broad and husky; and his voice was mild, rather than deep-throated. But he was well dressed, he had steely blue eyes, and he exuded charm. His jaw jutted in front of him like a beacon (having a chin that fell away from my mouth I was always impressed by a big, firm jaw).

Jack's entrance into the house was dramatic. Bubeh was waiting for him and he greeted her first with a long embrace while she murmured Yiddish words of thanks to God. Jack cried, Bubeh cried, and Lillian, Frances, Aunt Bess and I cried. Then the prodigal embraced

Mother, was introduced to us, and expressed proper delight at the way we looked.

Uncle Jack took special note of me. I was tall and skinny, but Jack told me that I looked like a man of eighteen and that my hand had a soldier's grip. I enlisted in his camp immediately.

We all went downstairs to the family dining room and had tea and lots of home-made pastry, over which Jack exclaimed. He talked about the raspberry jam that he'd dreamed of having with his tea. He remembered from his youth that raspberry jam was a panacea for all ills, and he told Bubeh that many times when he was sick in Mesopotamia he had prayed for raspberry jam.

This touching tale brought forth additional tears, particularly from Aunt Bessie, who was quick to cry. She would cry at funny stories because they were so adorable or at sad stories because they were so moving. She cried when you said goodbye or hello. She cried before the Sabbath because it was on the way, and after the Sabbath because it was gone. The wonderful thing about Aunt Bessie's crying was that in an effort to control the uncontrollable she would always smile; her face was always merry at the saddest times in her life. She knew she was a crybaby, but she would shrug, smile and say, "What can I do? I cry."

As Uncle Jack talked and ate he kept looking at all of us. Once in a while he would stop and repeat one of our names—just the name. "Belle," he would say as he looked at my mother, and he would shake his head in joy. Then, "Bessie," or "Lillian," or "Frances." But the tenderest of all looks and sounds was when he said *"Mammeh."* Each time he did, Aunt Bessie's tears fell and Lil observed jokingly, "There go the waterworks."

After a while Mother sent us children out of the room so that she and Bess and Bubeh could have grown-up talk with Uncle Jack. Upstairs Lillian, Frances and I discussed our long-lost relative. Lil thought he was marvelous. "He has a wonderful voice, like an actor. And did you notice his hands—manicured, yet strong and masculine?"

I too was captivated by Jack and was surprised and annoyed when Frances expressed reservations. She probably knew more about his past than either of us, but she didn't give us any additional information. However, she did say something about the Fifth Commandment; it sounded very mysterious, and when I went to my prayer book and read "Honour thy father and thy mother," I guessed that Uncle Jack had done something extremely bad. But I reasoned that bygones were bygones; after all, the war was over, and as a hero he *had* honored his father and mother, and now he should be forgiven for past indiscretions.

Uncle Jack was to spend a few days at our house, and later I took him up to his bedroom. As he unpacked he talked to me of his adventures, and then—wonder of wonders—he showed me a revolver he had brought back from the war. I have no idea what kind it was, but it was a mean-looking weapon and Jack let me hold it for a minute. He had one or two photos of himself taken in Arabia, but no knickknacks or other items of interest. I was a little disappointed that he hadn't brought me a gift, but of course I said nothing.

Uncle Jack's clothes were packed neatly, and he was precise in everything he did. He moved lightly and smiled warmly as he asked me about my father and how I got along with Zaida. I told him how I tried to cheat

with the *t'filin*. Jack told me that he had never had
his bar mitzvah. When I asked him why not, he said
it was a long story and he'd tell me about it another
time.

I asked him if he had killed anyone in the war and
he said, "Yes, I've shot some Turks and some Germans.
Once I killed a man with a bayonet."

"How?"

He laughed. "By sticking it in his belly."

I winced, and he changed the subject: Was I an
athlete? Though I was always interested in sports, I had
never been much good at any of them. I told Uncle
Jack that I played a little baseball and could run a long
distance.

"Well, you're still a kid," he said.

There was only one sport at which I was fairly
adept, I told Uncle Jack; my brother Sam had given me
some skill and polish in boxing.

"Good," he said. "One of these days we'll put on
the gloves and see how good you are."

When we went downstairs Jack said he'd like to
take us all to see a show. Mother and Bubeh didn't want
to go and Frances said she was tired. But Lil and I
went with him to Proctor's Palace, where we saw a
vaudeville bill featuring Jimmy Hussey, a great Jewish
comedian who was actually an Irishman, and Joe How-
ard, who sang his theme song, "I Wonder Who's Kissing Her Now."

Lillian and I loved Proctor's Palace; it was the
grandest vaudeville showplace in Newark. A friend, Al
Colombo, played cello in the orchestra, and often he
would take us backstage to meet some of the stars. At
various times we were introduced to such famous en-

tertainers as Belle Baker, Fanny Brice, the Mandel Brothers, George Jessel and the Courtney Sisters. While we also saw the plays that came to Newark, we enjoyed most the gaiety and music of the Palace. We knew the routines of Wellington and Cross, Moran and Mack, and the Avon Comedy Four, and our repertoire of imitations included Lewis and Dody, Eddie Foy, the Marx Brothers and Joe Cook.

That night we went backstage again with Al Colombo, who was pleased to meet Uncle Jack, and we all shook hands with Leon Navarro, a pianist-entertainer, who had once visited Schary Manor. Uncle Jack was modest about his war experiences with these new acquaintances, but Lillian and I basked in reflected glory. Afterward we went to an ice cream parlor, and on the way home Jack told us of shows he had seen in London and "Paree" and Arabia. He said that we were too young to hear about some of the things he had witnessed. This piqued Lil's interest, but Jack refused to talk.

When we got home Father and Mother were waiting up for us. Father had just come home from an Elk's convention in Atlantic City. He and Jack greeted each other heartily, and I noticed that after they embraced, Jack stepped back, took a long look and said, "Hugo."

The next day Elsie and Sam came home. They had been on the road; Sam was selling a service to employers designed to fight the I.W.W. by a series of patriotic pamphlets, cards, posters and pep talks. He had been doing very well and his tour of duty had taken him as far west as Omaha. They had arrived in New York that day, and when they heard that Jack was in town, hurried over to see him. Sam, ten years older than I, remembered Jack, but Elsie was new to the family and

Jack made a pretty speech wishing her happiness and good fortune.

During the day other relatives kept dropping in to see Jack: Aunt Mae and her husband Mike, with their children; Aunt Jennie and her husband Eppie; Aunt Anna, who lived with us (she was the only spinster left of Pa's five sisters, and from the way she kept brushing off possible *shiddukhs*—matchmaker's proposals—it appeared she would never marry); and Zaida's sister. By the time Aunt Clara and Uncle Sam arrived with their children, Lillian and Isadore, I began to detect changes in Jack. His conversation was less eloquent and his charm less charming. Finally he said that he had a headache and asked if I'd bring some hot tea to his room. Sam escorted him upstairs.

When I arrived with the tea, Jack was relaxed across his bed. He and Sam were laughing, and he told me that he'd had to get away from "the mob downstairs." "Relatives," he said, "can get to be a big pain in the behind."

While I agreed in principle, it occurred to me that after all the years he'd been away he might have been more gracious about them. But now the two of them were talking shop. He was going to settle down, Jack said, for a long spell. He wanted roots, a place, a home. Then he said, "I hear you have been teaching the kid how to handle the gloves."

Sam said, "I've been trying, but he'll never make it."

Jack asked me to get the gloves out; he wanted to see for himself. We cleared a small space. When we squared off, I realized that I was at least three inches taller than Jack and that I had at least that much reach on him. We danced around for a while, Jack making jokes and playing it cool and easy. But after a minute or so I knew he didn't know much about boxing. His right hand was kept too low and his left hand was too loose. He kept urging me to try and hit him and finally, tired of the prodding, I decided to experiment. I feinted a right, which opened up his stomach, and then jabbed my left into his ribs. He danced away, but he didn't like what I had done. "Powder-puff puncher," he said.

I moved closer and this time feinted with two left jabs, then hit him in the ribs again with my left hand, and when his left dropped I crossed with my right and hit him solidly on the jaw. He had a lot of jaw and I hit most of it.

Uncle Jack rolled with the punch but I knew that I had hurt him because when he looked at me there was an icy glaze in those blue eyes. I was hit suddenly by a flurry of punches, ending with one that knocked me down and almost out.

Sam came over and pulled me to my feet. Jack was yanking off his gloves. "Not bad, kid," he said with a quick smile.

I didn't say anything. At that age I never cried any more when I was hurt, but my head was sore and my body felt bruised. I took the gloves off and went to my room to clean up. Sam followed me and closed the door. "Don't ever put on the gloves with Jack again," he said.

"You didn't have to tell me."

"I know about Jack," Sam said. "He plays for keeps. He has a mean temper."

This seemed a good opportunity to find out about Jack's past. Sam was evasive, but he told me that Jack had been in a reform school, that he had always gone with a tough gang, and that before he ran off to join the American army he had stolen some money from Zaida's wallet.

Knowing this, I could understand my grandfather's behavior better, and I was surprised when Zaida returned unexpectedly the next morning to see his son.

It was a stiff reunion. But Jack stayed on for a few more weeks, and on a couple of Friday nights he even went to temple with Zaida. Apparently this was his way of looking for roots. However, one day when I came home from school I learned that Uncle Jack had departed. Pa was furious about something—it had to do with money—but no one would tell me precisely what had happened.

Occasionally through the years we heard news of Uncle Jack. He was married, then divorced. He was in California, then in Massachusetts. He was in Canada, then in Oregon. Finally, many years later, he was killed in an automobile accident. But by then the women in his family had shed all the tears they had for him.

13

*Music for
Special Occasions*

I am convinced that my father's distaste for musicians was acquired during the years that Lil and I talked about our ambitions to work in the theatre. Pa was certain that our affection for the instrumentalists who played at Schary Manor was leading us down the road to corruption. Though he liked to sing and dance, believing that these were social attributes valuable to all gentlemen and ladies, he eyed sourly and with distaste musicians who came to play at weddings and banquets.

Pa was truly shocked when Ralph Reichenthal, a lawyer who had earned his tuition expenses by playing piano, gave up the law, changed his name to Ralph Rainger, and proceeded to become a composer of popular music. He was sorry for Ralph's family; they had been betrayed by a son who recklessly renounced a respectable profession in favor of one that reeked of instability and immorality.

Pa suffered other shocks when Charles Baum, another Schary Manor veteran of weddings and bar mitzvah celebrations, became a successful band leader in New York. Finally, when young Henry Keselik, a handsome and gifted pianist, changed his name to Henry King and went on to become a favorite of the college kids, Pa was desolate. He could tolerate Jerome Norton, who played the violin as a means of bolstering his income while he worked in a legitimate business, but for young men like Ralph and Charles and Henry to succumb to the lure of show business was a tragedy and a disgrace.

For these reasons Pa developed an irrational hostility toward all musicians, and his behavior toward lean and independent Moe Glickstein, one of a group of brothers who made a living as barbers and itinerant music teachers and musicians, was typical.

The Glicksteins had a barber shop on Broome Street near Springfield Avenue, and whenever I went to have my hair cut I was always impressed by the tasteful sign in their window propped between an American flag and three shaving mugs. Black letters outlined in gold were printed on a white background, and the sign gave evidence of a busy and happy life for the Glickstein brothers, who could do many things. The card in the window proclaimed for all of them: "Shaves, Haircuts, Cuppings, Violin Lessons and Music for Special Occasions."

The only mystery to me was "cupping." Eventually I came to know what it meant, and though it terrified me I didn't feel as strongly about the practice as I did about leeches, the application of which I had once seen on my grandfather when he was laid up with a backache. I almost fainted at the sight of the sleek, black bloodsuckers hanging onto Zaida's back.

Cupping wasn't as gruesome, but it looked dangerous. The cupper would arrive with dozens of little glass cups and an alcohol burner. A swift application of flame burned out the oxygen in the cup to make it stick on the skin. The afflicted area of lumbago or arthritis might take the combined pulling power of twenty cups, and when I first saw Moe Glickstein apply them all over my father's back I was sure they could never be removed except by tearing out hunks of his flesh. But when they were taken off they left only polka dots of purple and blue the size of silver dollars. My father always felt better, and he would be pleasant to Moe Glickstein and tell him he was a good cupper.

But after Moe left Pa always said the same thing: The Glicksteins were good barbers and excellent cuppers, but in the field of music they were *klezmers*—a Yiddish term of disdain for people who play music badly.

Before I was old enough to shave, Moe promised me that when the time came I too would have a shaving mug reserved for me in the bright display of gay mugs that covered part of one wall of the Glickstein barbershop. I always examined the mugs while waiting to get my hair cut. There was one for my father; his name, H. H. Schary, was printed in Old English script, the letters were painted in blue and gold, and above the name was a picture of an eagle in red, white, blue and gold.

Most of the names on the mugs were familiar to me: Reinfeld, Schwartz, Gold, Mosias, Kaufman, Beigelman, Reich and a host of others, all with different designs. Some had patriotic motifs as backgrounds for the names. Others had pastoral scenes painted on them. Some had religious symbols, such as the six-pointed star or the menorah, and a few had the owners' names printed both in English and Yiddish. Moe and I had determined that when I was ready for my mug, it would carry my name in red letters outlined in blue and that there would be nothing else on the white cup. The simplicity of the design would make it the most distinctive of all the mugs.

When Pa visited the barber shop he would joke with Moe, and his attitude was just as friendly when Moe visited him to do the cupping, but when Moe and his orchestra came to the Manor to play, their relationship changed completely. Each of them seemed to go out of his way to deliberately irritate the other. If the musicians made too much noise in tuning up their instruments, Pa would want to know why they were tearing down the house. If the piano wasn't moved to its correct position on the platform, Moe would tell Pa that he was a musician, not a janitor, and that he had no intention of pushing the piano where it belonged. If it was a wet night out, Pa would warn the Glicksteins when they arrived not to muddy up the rugs with their dirty rubbers. If there wasn't a stand near the piano with a pitcher of water and glasses, Moe would insist that he and his colleagues were artists who had to be treated with deference. If Pa called Moe a *klezmer,* Moe would say Pa was nothing but a kosher head waiter. When Pa told Moe he was playing too fast or too slowly,

Moe told Pa to mind his business. If Pa ordered a lively tune, Moe would play a waltz; if he played a fox trot, Pa would tell him to play a tango. When Pa had to make an announcement and would ask for "a roller of the drums," Moe would oblige with a long series of sounds ending with cymbal crashes, and Pa would say, "I didn't ask you for a concerta." (He never said "concerto"; he thought "concerta" was more elegant.)

All of these exchanges were rancorous, but they never grew to the point of physical violence. And when the time came for the celebration of my parents' twenty-fifth wedding anniversary in 1921, Moe Glickstein was hired to play music for this special occasion.

There were six players in the band that night. There was Moe at the violin, a pianist, a drummer, a clarinetist, a cornetist and a saxophonist. Pa had a list of his favorite songs, tunes that meant something to Mother and himself, and he went over them with Moe when the orchestra arrived. Moe didn't have the music for some of the tunes, so Pa began to sing the melodies for him. "Listen to him," said Moe. "A regular Caruso."

"If you could play as good as I sing," said Pa, "you could close your barber shop and make a living as a musician, you *klezmer*."

It was a beautiful affair. The banquet room had been laid for a hundred guests and it was decorated with silver leaves and white satin swags draped from the chandeliers. A huge white paper bell with a silver clapper was suspended from the center of the ceiling. The staff at Schary Manor had relieved Mother of all her duties, and Fleischer, our chief cook, and his aides, Rabinowitz and Greenberg, outdid themselves with the meal. Frank and Sidney had chosen the best and handsomest waiters and they were all dressed in full-dress suits rented from Louis Lesser. Cozzolino and Sons, the printers who did most of our work, had printed up a lovely souvenir menu, which was their gift for the celebration.

Father had insisted that for this night we all had to have new clothes. Before the festivities began, he gave Mother her anniversary present, an exquisite diamond bar pin set in platinum. The guests included all the family of uncles and aunts and cousins except Uncle Max and Aunt Bessie. Pa and Max had had a terrible quarrel over money and had sworn that they would never speak to each other again. They never did. This was a blow to Mother and to us, not because of Uncle Max, whom none of us cherished, but because it meant we couldn't see Aunt Bessie or her children, Sam and Belle, whom we loved. But Mother and Bessie spoke to each other on the telephone that night and had a good cry.

Included in the guest list were old friends: the Lassers, the Goldfarbs, the Millers, and former Mayors Archibald and Gillen of Newark. There were lawyers (Pa loved lawyers) and doctors, including Drs. Nash, Hirshberg and Danzis, who had brought all of us children into the world. Also our boarders, the Kridels, Mr. Londau, Grace Lewis, Mrs. Goetz and two brothers named Haas who had moved in directly after the war. And of course there were Rabbis Brodsky, Silberfeld and Hoffman, who were most often the officiating rabbis at Schary Manor weddings.

Everybody was dressed to the nines.

After the meal (our top twenty-dollar-a-couple dinner), my brother Sam got up to act as master of ceremonies. There were telegrams to be read, including one from the governor of New Jersey. Lillian sang "Look for the Silver Lining," "When You Come to the End of a Perfect Day" and "Silver Threads Among the Gold." Frances spoke. So did I. Finally Father rose to his feet to acknowledge the toasts and compliments. He spoke about his happy life and his wife and his children; being capable of eloquent sentimentality, he soon had everyone—including himself—in tears.

Then the party adjourned to the ballroom, where Moe Glickstein and his orchestra struck up the first dance. It was "Let Me Call You Sweetheart," and Pa began the activities by dancing with Mother, while we all applauded. After the exhibition Zaida clapped his hands for attention. A wedding reception was meaningless without a kazatsky, he announced, and instantly Moe and his group blared the exciting strains of the traditional music, and Zaida started the dance. Seventy at the time, he was still erect and strong. Taking Mima Hindman for his partner (Bubeh had died a year before), he crossed his arms and kicked his heels and pranced proudly in the space cleared for the dance. When Mother and Father joined in, I was surprised that they were so good, for I had never seen them dance like this.

Moe and his combination swung into a Jewish tune and Ma and Pa began to do the Broygez, a wedding dance performed by the bride and groom. The man dances as if courting the lady. She rejects his advances by being broygez (angry). The dance requires moving in rhythm, stamping and turning, and it concludes with the clutching of a handkerchief as the couple kiss in a gesture of sweet surrender. Father and Mother were wonderful.

There was more applause and everybody decided to rest before they all got indigestion. It was a gay evening. Father was more even-tempered than we had seen him in months—he didn't even criticize Moe's music. There was more dancing, Lil sang some popular songs, and I recited "Gunga Din" and "Boots" (highly inappropriate, but Mother loved to hear me do the Kipling poems). As a surprise encore I recited the "To be, or not to be" soliloquy from *Hamlet*. When I finished, Uncle Mike yelled for me to go back to "Gunga Din." On later reflection I decided this was an implied and accurate criticism.

Before we realized it, people were saying goodnight. When Pa became aware of the hour, he called for "a roller on the drums." For once Moe obliged with no trimmings. Pa said that before anybody left he wanted to mention one thing he had forgotten to speak about at the dinner. First he thanked all the staff for what they had done to make the evening such a happy one; then he added, "I want to thank one man who has been so important tonight. He is a man who sometimes gets me angry, but tonight he outdid himself. I promise that I will never again call him a *klezmer*. Ladies and gentlemen, thanks to my friend, a gentleman and a scholar and a good musician, Moe Glickstein." The tribute overwhelmed Moe; he grew teary and dried his eyes with the sweaty handkerchief he had worn under his fiddle.

When everyone had gone, the family sat together and looked at Mother's bar pin and the gifts the guests had brought. The last box, a small one, was from Moe Glickstein and his wife. It was a silver Kiddush cup for wine, and the enclosed card read, "With love and respect to Belle and Hugo Schary from their favorite klezmer, Moe Glickstein."

Never again did Pa and Moe have a harsh word. But unfortunately, by the time I started shaving two months later, the Glicksteins had given up their barber shop. I never did get my shaving mug.

14

After You, Elias

My maternal grandparents, Bubeh and Zaida, were an important part of my life. (It was Bubeh, for instance, who taught me Kria'th Shma, the Hebrew bedtime prayer.) Bubeh and Mother were very close, and like Mother, Bubeh was an excellent cook and a good storyteller.

Once when I asked them about Uncle Jack, Bubeh reminded Mother of the story about a *shammes* (sexton) who was looking for work. So Mother told the yarn about a man who applied for the job of *shammes* at a synagogue. When he was asked to state his qualifications he said, "I am an expert accountant and I keep good accounts of all contributions and expenses."

This pleased the prospective employers and they asked if he had other talents.

"Naturally," he said. "I was once head painter of

an opera house. I know how to keep a place clean. I can manage servants and I do carpenter's work."

"What else?" they asked.

"Also, I am a former *chazan* [cantor] and I can sing like a bird. I know all the chants and the Torah by heart."

Overcome by this flood of talents, the committee wanted to know if the applicant had anything more to say.

"Yes," he said, "you should know this about me. I have only one fault."

"What's that?"

"On me you can't depend."

When Mother finished, Bubeh said ruefully, "That's your Uncle Jack."

Bubeh was also the family interpreter of dreams. When we told her we had dreamed of fire, she would say, "Ah, that's a good dream. Life is going to be bright for you." If we dreamed of dying, it was a sign of long life. A dream of drowning meant that good fortune would flow like water. A dream of an accident was a sign that ill luck was broken for us.

When Lillian became older, she finally confronted Bubeh with the fact that we all knew she was giving us only happy interpretations. Bubeh laughed and said, "Never tell your dreams to anybody except a smart person, because a fool will tell you what he thinks is the truth."

To Bubeh life was an adventure, and all signs and omens were good ones. Friday the thirteenth was a day she looked forward to; it meant that something good was going to happen. When Mother was elected presi-

dent of the Women's Auxiliary of the Israel Home for
the Aged on Friday the thirteenth, Bubeh was vindi-
cated. We children soon lost any respect for most super-
stitions because of Bubeh's affirmative attitude toward
life.

Bubeh watched over and cared for Zaida in old-
world fashion. They had been married in 1868, when
Zaida was eighteen and Bubeh sixteen. Together they
had endured much, including pogroms, from which
they were saved by virtue of Zaida's service in the
Czar's army.

When Bubeh had her fatal heart attack in 1920, we
were all bereft. We worried about Zaida because he
was lonely and lost without the constant companionship
of a wife he had loved for fifty-two years. But Zaida,
helped by Mother and the rest of the family, tried to
keep to his daily routine in an effort to make life seem
normal. He would awake, say his prayers, have his
morning schnapps, eat his breakfast, and walk to temple. During the day he would read or work in the
Manor supervising the kosher aspects of the kitchen,
and at dusk he would go to temple again for the evening prayers.

The schedule was always the same. Zaida walked
to temple most of the time with an old friend he had
known in Russia, Elias Reich, who had also settled in
Newark and had sired a large family. Of his three sons,
one, Jack Reich, was our dentist, and the other two
were doctors. The two bearded old gentlemen, both
well groomed, walked on High Street to Kinney Street
and up Kinney to Prince Street where the Anshe Russia
Temple was located. They talked endlessly about their
families, about the Talmud, of the bygone days in Rus-

sia and of the incredible *medinah* (utopia) that was America.

Elias Reich was short and stocky; Zaida was long and lean. They were friendly with almost everyone in the neighborhood. On Kinney Street they occasionally stopped at Katchen's drugstore for a lemon phosphate, but that was about the extent of their outside pleasures. They were both widowers, and in each other's bereavement they found a strong bond of friendship.

One night a heavy rain began to fall as they left the temple to walk home. The rain, following on the heels of a light snowfall, made the streets slippery and slushy. It was dark and the traffic on Kinney Street was heavy for a weekday night. Helping each other down the curb, Elias and Zaida were struck by a heavy truck that skidded into both of them, throwing them to the pavement.

A crowd of friends was leaving the temple, and in a moment Baruch and Elias were surrounded by clucking elders, who began to yell for an ambulance. Rabbi Brodsky was summoned from the temple and kneeled on the pavement to give comfort to the two men. Both of them were bleeding and obviously badly hurt, but the Beth Israel Hospital was only a few blocks away and an ambulance was on the scene in a matter of minutes. In it were Dr. Danzis and one of the Drs. Reich, who had been at the hospital when the call came in.

They found Zaida and Elias protected from the rain by friends who had formed a canopy of umbrellas over them and had shed overcoats to keep the patients as warm and dry as possible. Both victims were breathing heavily and in great distress. The first stretcher was made ready for Elias, who protested loudly, "No, first

Baruch." When Zaida heard this, he called out just as firmly, "No, after you, Elias."

Zaida and Elias were favorite characters of the neighborhood and their families were well known, so when the two friends arrived at Beth Israel, there was a congregation of doctors waiting for them. In addition to the other Reich boys, there were Drs. Aaron Parsonnet, Nash, Hirschberg and members of the hospital staff.

Examination revealed that Elias had a fractured shoulder, a concussion, a number of cracked ribs, countless abrasions and bruises and a cut on his forehead. Zaida had a like number of bruises, a badly cut head, a fractured collarbone and four broken ribs, two of them puncturing a lung.

At that time, 1921, Zaida was seventy-one years old and Elias a year older. The doctors were gloomy about their chances for recovery, but they went to work. In the meantime the families had gathered, and the lobby of the Beth Israel looked like a reunion of all the descendants of the Drachler and Reich clans.

Schary Manor was catering a charity dinner that night, and when the call came, Mother slipped a coat over her apron and rushed to the hospital with Pa, who told Fleischer and Sidney and Frank to carry on. Many of the guests at the charity banquet knew both families and the news buzzed through the hall. As the evening wore on, guests popped out to get bulletins—all of them bad.

After the dinner was over and I had checked out all the coats and hats, I raced to the hospital. By then Frances and Lillian were there, and when I saw their faces I knew Zaida was in serious trouble. Both men had been moved from the operating rooms to private rooms and were isolated from their unhappy families by a corps of doctors and private nurses. Rabbi Brodsky had come by to sit and pray. Elias and Baruch weren't merely members of his congregation; they were two dear friends and he was there to help, if help was needed. Mother was seated, holding her hands in characteristic fashion, the fingers of the right hand clutching the back of her left. When I kissed her she only nodded. Father was talking quietly to Dr. Danzis and Dr. Louis Reich, and there was much whispering and sobbing going on all over the lobby. In a moment Dr. Danzis came to my mother and took her hands. "Belle, dear, there is no point in waiting. He is still under ether. We will know more in the morning."

"What do you think, Max?"

"I can't say, Belle. They are both strong, but old. They are badly hurt. It's serious, Belle, very serious."

Mother nodded and Pa helped her up. I started to get a taxi, but the rain had stopped and Mother said she wanted to walk.

Back at the Manor, Fleischer, Frank, Sidney and Rosie Carter had waited up for us. They served us hot food and tea as we gave them the news. They shook their heads sadly—all except Rosie, who said, "He's a tough old bird, that Zaida. He's going to be all right."

We all seized on this note of optimism and reassured Mother. She nodded as if convinced, but it was clear that she wasn't. Then Pa got on the telephone and reported to all the uncles and aunts. As we went upstairs to bed, the boarders opened their bedroom doors and asked for the latest news. Mrs. Goetz was the only one who proved less than comforting; "It's a tragedy," she said. "Well, at least he'll be with his dear wife again." Then she asked me to get her a cup of tea and two slices of gluten bread.

When I got up the next morning, Mother had already been to the hospital. Both old men were being kept comfortable and there was no crisis. The day was a dreary one, but it passed quickly because there was work to do for another large affair that night. All day Mother got bulletins from the hospital, supplied by Pa and Lil and Frances. When the dinner was over, we all decided to go to bed early, but as we were preparing to turn in we received an urgent call from Dr. Danzis. There was a crisis and Zaida was in desperate difficulties.

Feter Dudy, Zaida's brother-in-law, who was pinch-hitting for him by keeping a watchful eye on the kitchen, went with us to the hospital. When we arrived, Dr. Danzis told Mother that Zaida's lungs were beginning to fill with fluid. For a man his age the condition looked hopeless.

We were allowed into Zaida's room. He was propped up in bed. His skin looked olive green, and there was a hoarse rattling sound to his breathing. His eyes were closed, his skull cap was perched on his head (they knew he would want it there under any circumstances), and his hands were spread out on the blanket. As I looked at him I remembered something that Bubeh had told me. She said that when a sick person spreads out his hands he is giving up life, but when he clenches his fists he is hanging on and fighting for life. It was terrible to see Zaida's hands spread out.

There was nothing to do; we just stood there. Mother was holding her left hand with her right, and

Pa had his arm around her. Finally Feter Dudy spoke.

"*Du shlofst,* Baruch?" (Are you asleep, Baruch?)

There was no sound in answer to Feter Dudy's absurd question except the hard, labored rattling sound of Zaida's breathing. Dr. Danzis came into the room and the nurse whispered to him and showed him a chart. He nodded solemnly. Suddenly Zaida stopped breathing, then began again even more slowly. After a minute or two he opened one eye—just one eye. He looked at us; we looked back at him. Then he opened his other eye and his head moved slowly around the room as his breathing continued heavy and loud. After giving all of us a baleful look, he muttered something which we didn't hear.

"*Vus hust du gezogt,* Totta?" (What did you say, Father?) Mother asked.

Zaida coughed, cleared his throat, opened his eyes wider, and said, quite clearly, "*Haldt sich ein. Ich shtarb nisht.*" (Hold everything. I'm not dying.)

Then Dr. Danzis shooed us out. When we got to the lobby Mother refused to leave, so Pa sent Lil, Frances and me back to the house.

The next morning Mother came home smiling. Zaida had meant what he said. He had coughed up the fluid, his fever had fallen, and despite the doctor's protest, he had ordered Mother to bring his phylacteries to the hospital so that he could resume his morning prayers as soon as possible. Elias too had made the turn. To the amazement of all the doctors, who finally attributed the miracle to the tough constitution of Russian Jews, the two friends recovered rapidly. After a few days they were shifted into a double room, where they picked up their interrupted dialogues.

Within a month Zaida and Elias had both healed completely and went to Lakewood to a kosher hotel for a week's recuperation. A week after they returned home they resumed their morning and evening walks to *shul*. Zaida was just as erect, tall and firm-gaited as before. He made only one concession to the doctors. He had always smoked Turkish cigarettes—Omars, Hassans or Turkish Trophies. When the doctors insisted that he cut his smoking in half, he agreed.

But I was watching one day as Zaida opened his cigarette case. His cigarettes had been cut in two equal parts. When I asked him why, he said, "I always keep a promise. I told the doctors I would cut my smoking in half—and that's exactly what I'm doing."

Zaida kept smoking and lived happily until his eighty-fourth year.

15

A Wreath for Rosie Carter

Rosie Carter worked for us for eight years. She came to the first Schary Manor at 584 High Street in 1914 and moved with us to No. 604, bringing along her assorted irons, white uniforms and authoritative manner. Rosie was a little under six feet tall and weighed almost two hundred pounds. Her skin was like polished ebony.

There was nothing of the Uncle Tom in Rosie. She had a fierce pride in her work, which carried a multitude of responsibilities. She was in charge of the Negro girls, their number varying from three to six, who worked in the pantry, and she insisted that their uniforms and hands be clean at all times. As the pantry chores progressed from skinning the fish to preparing fruit cocktail to chopping liver, Rosie moved the girls along to the sink. "Wash up, girls, we don't like the fruit to smell like fish."

Each new girl and pantryman received instructions from Rosie, for she knew all about kosher food. For instance, dishes used for dairy food must never be mixed with dishes used for meat; glasses are *parvehdik*, usable for all needs, because glass is not porous. On Passover, Rosie knew where and how to store the utensils used for the rest of the year, which under no circumstances were to be used during the holiday. She would say to Zaida as he came in to inspect, "Don't worry, Grandpa, everything is going to be absolutely *Pesachdik* (according to the rules prescribed for Passover).

Over the years Rosie had picked up a large Yiddish vocabulary. She spoke it with a warm, deep Southern accent, and her favorite joke was to say something in Yiddish like, "*Vus zogt ihr haynt?*" (What do you say today?), and then add, "you all." Rosie knew everything about us. She thought Father's tempers were inexcusable. She argued that he was a gentleman and it wasn't worthy of him to get so angry. She adored my mother and Bubeh and was always urging them to get rest: "Everything's all set; you go up and get some sleep." Like all of us, she worried about Frances, who was always so quiet.

My father called Frances "Faygele" (Little Bird), and while he whacked my brother Sam, Lillian and me for any kind of misbehavior, he never slapped Frances or even raised his voice to her. There was something serene about her, something that set her apart and above the rest of us. Sam was restless and eager to move on; Lillian was always volatile, and willing and able to be mother to the rest of the world; I was moody, with moments of extreme gregariousness followed by periods of self-isolation. But Frances was none of these things. She was always soft-spoken, sure of what she wanted and wise about the world. She was the least energetic of the Scharys, but she had the gift of using all her abilities without exhausting her capabilities. All of us had a special feeling about Frances, and whenever she was ill she received overwhelming care and attention from everyone in the house. Rosie, for instance, fussed over her as if she were a small child. Sometimes this annoyed me, but if I protested, Rosie would give me a sharp look and say, "Now that's no way for a nice Jewish boy to act."

Through the years we met most of Rosie's family, over whom she ruled like an Ethiopian queen. She never married, but she had countless nieces and cousins and sisters who were always being married or getting involved with men. Once when one of the swains arrived to continue an unwelcome liaison with one of her nieces, Rosie ordered him out of the pantry. We were making fruit salad at the time and all of us were busy slicing up oranges and grapefruit and pineapple. The young buck, who had prepared himself for the rendez-vous by having a few drinks, refused to leave. Without a word Rosie hit him over the head with a soaking wet towel that she had folded into a weapon. She laid it around the young man's head and shoulders like a mace until John, our Polish porter, arrived, murmured his eternal "Sonamonbitch," and heaved the intruder out the back door.

In addition to all of Rosie's other chores and duties, she reserved for herself the pleasure of laundering the family's handkerchiefs. Once I asked her why she liked to wash and iron only handkerchiefs. She told me that washing and ironing gave her a sense of serenity and order, and since handkerchiefs were small and simple to iron, she was able to achieve peace without thought.

Rosie was incorruptibly honest. If there was leftover food, she never assumed that any of it was hers. If she found a penny on the floor, it went into the small charity box in the kitchen which Mother had installed for the Israel Home for the Aged. If any one of the help filched as much as a chicken leg, Rosie would bounce him out of the house. For this reason we were surprised and puzzled after a long time when we became aware that we were losing handkerchiefs.

My Aunt Anna, who was living in the house with us, had given me a silk pongee handkerchief for my fifteenth birthday. It was the first elegant handkerchief I had ever owned. After it had been laundered once I decided to reserve it for some extra-special evening. One night, when I was going to a block dance with Elizabeth Jay, I couldn't find it anywhere. Rosie was vague. "Oh, yes, I remember it when you first got it, but not since then." When I asked Father if my pongee was mixed up with his, he looked and said no, but remarked that his own supply seemed very low.

I stewed and nagged about my loss for days until Mother finally told me to forget it and stop talking about it. I was, and still am, particular about laundry, because when we were poor most of my handkerchiefs, shirts, and pajamas were shoddy—clean but shoddy. Most of my shirts were my father's or brother's, which had been cut down to fit me when the collars and cuffs gave out. As a result, when I began to accumulate belongings of my own, I watched over them like a hawk. So when Mother told me to forget about my pongee handkerchief, I didn't—I just stopped talking about it.

When I noticed that other handkerchiefs were gone, I didn't say a word; I just scurried about looking for them in Father's bureau or in Zaida's chest of drawers. Soon I began to suspect that John was stealing them, but since I didn't talk Polish and John had only his one English word, I let the matter drop.

One evening some months later when Lillian was going out with a boy she particularly liked, she asked Mother for a lacy handkerchief. What had happened to the Alençon lace one she had received as a Hanukkah present, Mother asked. Lil said that it was missing. Mother went to her bureau, found one that Lillian liked, and then went through the rest of her supply and found that some of *her* handkerchiefs were missing.

By now there was no doubt that somebody was rifling our supply of handkerchiefs. Some of us thought that the culprit was John; others believed that Rosie's niece Beulah was the thief and that Rosie was covering up for her. Pa surmised that Sidney might be handing them out as gifts to some of the waitresses in exchange for bedroom favors.

One Sunday in 1922 one of Rosie's sisters came to tell us that Rosie had had a heart attack the night before and had been rushed to the City Hospital. Since Rosie had never had a day's illness, this was like hearing that the Newark Courthouse had collapsed. Mother immediately telephoned someone at the hospital to verify the news, then called Dr. Nash to ask him to attend to Rosie.

There was a wedding party that night and Mother had a lot of work in the kitchen, but she told me to remind her when it was one o'clock; she would be able to take time off then and go to see Rosie. In the meanwhile she gave Rosie's sister some money to take care of any extra costs. At one o'clock I reminded Mother and she called the hospital again. After a moment she hung up the phone and said, *"Baruch dayan emes."* This means "Blessed be Thy judgment," and it is said when someone dies. Rosie was dead.

Mother told the family, then the other servants, and some of them departed immediately for Rosie's apartment to mourn and make arrangements. We were left short-handed, but Lillian, Frances and I pitched in with the pantry work and the wedding went off on schedule. After the party was over we sat in the kitchen and talked about Rosie. Father said that he and Mother would see to it that she had an appropriate funeral with a big floral wreath. She had always loved beautiful flowers.

On Monday morning Mother and I went to Rosie's apartment on Spruce Street. It was a poor neighborhood and the house was run-down, but Rosie's rooms, a bedroom, living room and kitchen, were neat and clean. Some of Rosie's relatives were there, and they were happy to see Mother and grateful for the help she offered. But it was not needed; Rosie had left money and a letter with complete instructions on how and where she was to be buried, as well as a small inheritance for her nieces and sisters and cousins.

Rosie was in her bedroom. She had been brought there according to the instructions expressed in her letter. She was stretched out on her bed, dressed in a black dress with white piping around the collar and cuffs; her hands were folded across her stomach and her thick mop of hair had been carefully combed. I saw all this in a moment. Then my eyes ranged across the room to her dresser. There, heaped in huge stacks, were dozens and dozens of handkerchiefs, carefully arranged and properly laundered and folded. On top of one of the stacks was my long-lost pongee.

I don't know what I felt first—joy at finding my handkerchief or shock at realizing that Rosie had been taking the missing items for all those years. I know that Mother saw the pile on the bureau too, but she didn't look at me and she said nothing.

Rosie's sister had come into the room and Mother asked her when and where the funeral was to be. Then we said goodbye and Rosie's sister escorted us out to the street.

"It's a funny thing, Mrs. Schary," she said. "You know Rosie never took anything that wasn't hers."

"I know," Mother said.

I kept my mouth shut.

"But," Rosie's sister went on, "she loved handkerchiefs. And it was the only thing she did that was wrong. 'Some day,' she said to me, 'I'm going to give them all back.' She'd wash them out every few weeks to keep them clean and new. She said it was like having part of all of you living with her."

To an adolescent boy this all seemed very weird, and later I asked Mother if she was going to take back the handkerchiefs. She said that they had meant so much to Rosie that it would be like stealing if we took them back. As I thought about it, I knew she was right. I felt terribly sorry for Rosie and sad that she was gone, and I also felt like a fool for worrying so much about that small square of silk pongee.

16

Remember, the Dishes
Aren't Paid For Yet

From the day Pa bought the first Schary Manor, he was possessive and paternalistic about his place of business. As we prospered and moved to the larger Manor at 604 High Street, these attitudes became even more pronounced. Each dish, fork, knife, glass, banquet chair and napkin was *his*. They belonged to him, they were owned by him, and he brooked no carelessness with his possessions. If a napkin was torn he would rip it to shreds and toss it away; but no other person had that right.

Pa would walk through the dining room before dinner was served and check each place setting. The napkins were folded according to the cost of the menu. The cheapest menu was identified by a simple folded napkin beside the plate. Higher-priced affairs were graced by napkins folded like baskets, with a roll inside each. The most expensive dinners were resplendent with napkins arranged to look like flowers. This last was of Father's own design, and he worked for a long time to teach the intricate folding to Sidney, Frank and Rosie. (All of them hated the extra effort; they claimed that the napkins looked more like white artichokes than flowers.) Lillian and Frances helped out on these extra-special occasions and would spend the better part of the day getting the napkins ready.

As Pa patrolled the dining room he would occasionally spot a dish with a crack in it. Instantly he would shout for Frank or Sidney. "How many times have I yelled till my lungs got tired that I don't want cracked dishes?"

If Frank was feeling particularly sassy, he'd answer, "The first time I ever heard you say that was just now."

Pa would take the dish and split it. "Cracks in dishes hide bugs that give you diseases. Get another dish." Then he would hand the fragments to Frank and continue his rounds. If Pa found a cracked dish when we were eating alone, much the same dialogue would take place, and my mother and we children would get a lecture on cleanliness, bugs and health until he had cracked the dish and the meal could go on.

Mother was always sympathetic to Pa's fetish for order, but she would point out to him that while it was true that he owned everything, the people who came to eat and celebrate had certain rights, among them the privilege of being able to eat as they pleased. She was touching a particularly sore point, for once dinner had started, Pa felt that it was *his* privilege to correct the eating habits of some of the people who found their way into our banquet rooms.

He was good-humored about it, especially if he knew the offender. He would stop and smile. "Hymie, I'm surprised. Didn't you hear about the fellow who cut his tongue eating with his knife?" Or, "If you sit up straight when you eat, you'll never get an ulcer. It's true. Dr. Nash told me."

Most of the time Father got away with this corrective bantering but sometimes there was trouble, as on the night the Goldenbergs had a party to mark their twenty-fifth anniversary. It was a magnificent affair, for the Goldenbergs had made a lot of money manufacturing mattresses. Their wedding anniversary was on Washington's Birthday, and like most American Jews, they took great pride in combining their personal lives with events in American history. The fact that February 22 was the birthday of the Father of Our Country produced some elaborate toasts at the beginning of the dinner. And the fact that the Goldenbergs had spawned eleven children during their twenty-five years together inspired the toastmaster (Goldenberg's brother, a lawyer) to such flights of comic rhetoric as, "We come here tonight to celebrate the birthday of the Father of Our Country and to raise our glasses to two wonderful people, Joe and Adele Goldenberg, who picked up where George Washington left off."

The inevitable reaction to gay toasts and funny telegrams, which were usually given or read before the meal, was laughter and applause, and if they were especially delighted, the audience would rap on the dishes with their knives or hammer at the glasses with their spoons.

Pa's response was equally predictable. He would hurry over to the musicians' platform, calling out to the leader of the band as he approached, "Quick, give me a roller on the drums." The drummer would hit the snare drum and end with a crash of the cymbals. Pa would lift up his hands, his face bright with a wide smile, looking for all the world as though he were about to give a benediction.

"Ladies and gentlemen." There would be applause, which my father would acknowledge with "Thank you." Then he would continue, "We want you to have a good time. This is a shpectocular evening." (Pa always had trouble with the word "spectacular" too. When we corrected him he'd answer, "Please, I don't speak a high language, but I know enough words to make a living for my family. I don't have to take lessons.")

On the night of the Goldenberg affair Joe Goldenberg's brother was disconcerted by Pa's interruption, but he was helpless as Pa went on, "Mrs. Schary and I want you to have a good time, but please remember the dishes aren't paid for yet, so don't applause [he never used the verb 'applaud'] on the dishes with the silverware. Thank you. Enjoy your food—that's paid for."

Pa got a laugh and a good hand and there was no more banging on the dishes. Now in an expansive mood, he waved to Lawyer Goldenberg, who continued with his speech. The three hundred guests were having a fine time, and when the toast was over they all dug into their grapefruit, which sported tiny American flags as a patriotic reminder.

I was standing facing the main table, which was on a dais over which had been hung a large picture, purportedly of George and Martha Washington. Hanging right next to it was a flattering picture of Joe and Adele Goldenberg. These had been the surprise decorations furnished by the employees of Goldenberg and Sons, Manufacturers of Fine Mattresses. My father had stopped at a nearby table to exchange pleasantries with some of the guests.

Our circular tables usually seated eight. At one time Pa had created a slogan, "Schary Manor, Where You Get a Square Meal on a Round Table," but fortunately one of the boarders in our home, George Kridel, whom Pa respected as "an elegant gentleman," talked him out of it after the rest of us had failed to budge him. At the next table was seated a heavy-set man, who, I learned later, was "in the iron business," a euphemistic term for "junkman." He was a red-faced, red-haired gentleman, who obviously had had many drinks before dinner. With him was his wife, who was as husky as her husband, and three other couples, all of whom were having a grand evening of it. The fish dish was being served and the junkman was about to plow into it when Pa approached him and suggested that since it was a formal dinner party, it might be better to keep his napkin on his lap instead of tucking it into his collar. The junkman said that my father had a big nose and that he shouldn't stick it into everybody's business. With that, he banged on the glass with his spoon for emphasis. Pa became polite. "I'm sorry, sir, I didn't want to offend you. But please don't bang on the glasses." He tried to smile, but there was no heart in it. "They aren't paid for yet."

The junkman said he hated lousy jokes and continued hitting the glass. Pa became excessively formal,
and I bowed a familiar warning to Sidney, who headed
toward the table. Whenever we pointed to Pa and then
bowed, it meant only one thing: the head of the house
was about to explode.

"As I asked you, mister, I would appreciate it extremely if you wouldn't bang on the glasses," Pa said
icily. "And please put your napkin in your lap."

At this point the junkman made a serious error: he
told my father to go to hell. Pa reached over, plucked
the napkin out of the man's collar, and placed it in his
lap. The junkman then made his second serious mistake:
he picked up the glass and threw the water at Pa.
Pa hit him. The junkman's wife got up and hit Pa with
her purse. Sidney pulled her away, and when the junkman got up and rushed at Pa, the host of Schary Manor
clobbered him with a right hand and the junkman fell
to the floor.

By now the Goldenberg's twenty-fifth anniversary
party was in danger of becoming a Jewish Donnybrook.
But Moe Glickstein, the leader of the orchestra, had
played at Schary Manor many times and knew what to
do when Father lost his temper. In an instant the band
was playing "The Star-Spangled Banner." Those guests
not already on their feet stood up. The ones who were
already up were halted in their tracks. As the band
played loud and long, my mother, summoned from the
kitchen, escorted Father out of the dining room and
into the office.

The junkman's wife and friends, aided by Sidney
and me, helped him into the washroom upstairs. His
nose was bleeding and he was swearing that he would

kill Pa. When the toastmaster, Lawyer Goldenberg, came upstairs he quieted the bleeding man, who said he wanted to go home. Lil checked out his coat and hat, along with all the garments belonging to his family and friends (and was annoyed that they didn't leave her a tip).

I went down to the office. Father was sitting in his oak swivel chair and Mother was standing over him. "Are you crazy, Hugo?" I heard her say as I came into the office.

After one of his sudden bursts of violence, Father was always white-faced and his voice was low and quiet. "Listen, Belle, I'm not crazy. At Schary Manor people should eat like gentlemen."

My mother had an answer for that. "You know what they say about Schary Manor? At Schary Manor, Hugo Schary hits you in the face."

Before Pa could comment, Lawyer Goldenberg walked into the office. "Schary," he said, "Mr. Kaiser intends to sue you for assault and battery. You should be ashamed of yourself."

Pa was equal to this charge. He stood up and with quiet dignity and righteousness answered, "*You* should be ashamed. On an occasion like this you shouldn't invite tramps like that."

"Mr. Kaiser is no tramp."

"He's a junkman," said Pa.

"Please, Mr. Goldenberg," said Mother, "go back and try and enjoy the rest of the dinner. We're very sorry. I'm sure Mr. Kaiser will be all right, and my husband will apologize to him tomorrow."

"My tongue will fall off before I apologize to that tramp."

"Do you know," said Mr. Goldenberg, "that Kaiser is a thirty-second-degree Mason?"

Pa, a member of the Elks, had also started his apprenticeship in the Masons, so this intelligence impressed him. Weakly he countered, "A thirty-second-degree Mason shouldn't drink."

"Listen, Schary, all I can tell you is that your temper is bad for your business. And if Kaiser has you arrested, it will serve you right. If it wasn't for your wife, we would cancel our son's bar mitzvah party."

Mother spoke up. "Mr. Goldenberg, my husband and I run Schary Manor. While we would like to cater your son's bar mitzvah, we don't want and don't need charity."

Mr. Goldenberg was a kind man and he apologized for his last remark. His good manners captivated Pa, who then apologized to Mr. Goldenberg. Soon Goldenberg admitted that Kaiser was a boor and that he was invited only because he was a cousin of Mrs. Goldenberg's sister-in-law. Finally everybody shook hands, and Lawyer Goldenberg went back to the party. When Mother suggested that Pa go to my Uncle Mike's house and play pinochle, he agreed; he could use some relaxation, he said. I went back to my post in the dining room and Mother returned to the kitchen. Sidney had cleared away the empty table, and when I came in and told him that all was well he said, "In a free-for-all fight I'd bet on that guy's wife. She's got a kick like a mule."

By now we were serving the roast chicken, and the guests were enjoying the celebration and Glickstein's band was playing "Japanese Sandman."

Pa came home as the last guest was leaving. He'd had some fine relaxation and was ahead thirty dollars.

As he closed the door behind him, he turned to my mother and kissed her. "Belle," he said, "you are a good wife. I was so proud that you took my side against Goldenberg. I make you a promise. Never again will I hit another guest in Schary Manor."

The promise pleased Mother, and beyond one incident three years later, Father kept his bargain. But even in that instance—a drunken bootlegger had slapped a woman—he rushed the man outside before hitting him, thus keeping his word by not making the assault *in* the Manor.

17

Who's the Rabbi?

When arrangements were being made for a wedding at Schary Manor, the first question we always asked was, "Who's the rabbi?" The answer was important, because, thanks to our years of experience, we could determine from it the kind of ceremony there would be. Each rabbi had his own form of service, his own distinctive style, and his own idea about the length of the ceremony. Rabbi Brodsky's rituals ran the longest, Rabbi Hoffman of the Oheb Sholem was runner-up, Rabbi Julius Silberfeld of B'Nai Abraham followed, and Rabbi Solomon Foster of B'Nai Jeshurun, a reform congregation, had the shortest services.

Not only was each rabbi different, but there was also an unspoken competition which reflected the rivalry between the congregations. This, in turn, reflected the differences in the layers of Jewish life in Newark.

Rabbi Brodsky, who had been with the Anshe Russia temple since its foundation, was the chief orthodox rabbi and the dean of the Newark rabbinate. He was a handsome model of the traditional Eastern European rabbi: tall and dignified, with a long, wispy white beard, which hung in splendid display almost to his waist. With firmness and authority he represented the active orthodox Russian-Jewish community of the city; most of the weddings or bar mitzvahs or Bris Milahs (circumcision ceremonies) celebrated by Russian Jews were presided over by Reb Brodsky. His wedding services were lengthy and ritualistic. A good part of them were in Yiddish and Hebrew, only a small part in English, and he always concluded with the words, "Now kiss your bride and be happy."

Members of synagogues never hesitate to criticize their rabbis. They point out that if Abraham had the privilege of debating a point with God as reported in the Book of Genesis, then they certainly have the right to mention to a rabbi anything that displeases them. As I have mentioned earlier, Zaida disliked Reb Brodsky's rather roguish conclusion to the wedding ceremony; he believed it was too commonplace for a great rabbi like Brodsky—and of course he expressed his displeasure. Reb Brodsky listened because he had respect for Zaida's opinions. He stroked his beard, sipped his tea, nodded his head—and then ignored Zaida's criticism.

Israel Lipkin, a famous Lithuanian novelist, once wrote, "A rabbi whom they don't want to drive out of town isn't a rabbi, and a rabbi whom they actually drive out isn't a man." So while Brodsky had critics, as do all members of the clergy, he would sort out the criticisms and make up his own mind. He remained a man and stayed in the pulpit of Anshe Russia till the end of his long and active life.

Rabbi Hoffman of the Oheb Sholem was another towering figure. He was tall and heavier than Rabbi Brodsky and had a black spade beard and a deep mellifluous voice that rolled out the ancient Hebrew prayers with awesome authority. His congregation was largely German-Jewish, and they had a rather snobbish attitude toward the Russian Jews. This was an old-world antipathy, brought over and maintained in America. The congregation of Oheb Sholem was richer and gave generously to all charity campaigns. Though they observed the holidays in the traditional ways, there was a difference: a service in Oheb Sholem might have all the same words, but the sound of devotion was never as loud or as passionate as that in the Anshe Russia.

Rabbi Hoffman's ceremonies exuded dignity and a tone of solemnity, which was undoubtedly due in part to the rabbi's ministerial rather than patriarchal appearance. My father once said, "You feel you could tell a good joke to Brodsky, but you would never try and tell one to Hoffman." There were critics too of Rabbi Hoffman, but most of his congregation weren't public in their judgments. They were afraid that outsiders would repeat their opinions and that it might reflect badly on their rabbi, to whom they were as devoted as the Anshe Russians were to Brodsky.

Rabbi Silberfeld, a comparative newcomer at the time, was a younger man than Brodsky and Hoffman and a new and different type of leader. He wore no beard, only a mustache, which he assumed made him look older. His eyes had a gay and merry look. His congregation, B'Nai Abraham, was an amalgam of Russian Jews on the way out of orthodoxy into conservatism and German Jews who were resisting the drive into reform Judaism but didn't relish the orthodoxy of Anshe Russia that was so typically Eastern European and old-world.

All of these congregants found a new home and a new rabbi in B'Nai Abraham, and the congregation prospered. Rabbi Silberfeld had a flair for wedding ceremonies; where Brodsky's were long and sometimes incomprehensible to the less learned Jews, and where Hoffman's were a bit pedantic and solemn, Silberfeld brought pace and warmth and intelligibility as well as religion to his ceremonies. So he thrived and soon earned the title of "The Marrying Rabbi." In a short time he was outrunning Brodsky and Hoffman and his congregation was outstripping the others in acquiring new members. Silberfeld brought energy to his duties and a faster tempo more attuned to the times of his congregation. But he too had his critics, among them Zaida, who didn't believe in a rabbi who didn't wear a beard. Also, Zaida believed that Silberfeld was making religion too easy. "It's not easy to be a Jew," argued Zaida. "It's hard. And if you make it too easy, you won't be a good Jew."

Our family shifted membership to B'Nai Abraham —but not Zaida. He stayed with the Anshe Russia, and while he professed to believe that my mother preferred the new temple because the women sat with the men in the more modern fashion, he thought that Ma and Pa were becoming lazy in their religious devotions. Of course he didn't think it made any difference where I went to *shul;* he had long renounced the chance of my becoming a *talmid* (scholar).

Rabbi Foster was the master of the flock of the B'Nai Jeshurun congregation, which represented the drift of the Jewish brethren in Newark to Reform Judaism. Even those of us in the family who knew little about our faith and didn't take it as seriously as Zaida had misgivings about going into a temple and uncovering our heads. The services in the B'Nai Jeshurun were largely in English and thus were more intelligible, but they lacked the sound of piety to which we had become accustomed. Zaida wouldn't even discuss the B'Nai Jeshurun; as far as he was concerned, it might as well be a church. His feelings were one more reflection of the swirling tides of disagreement in Newark Jewish religious life. The reform movement was new and strange and was greeted with suspicion. Since at first the congregation was not large, the number of weddings over which Rabbi Foster presided was small, but when he did appear at Schary Manor we discovered that his ceremonies were crisp and intelligent. His sermons were more intellectual than the other rabbis', and though he was learned in Hebrew, the song of his prayers didn't compare to any of the other three. Last, his ceremonies were the shortest by at least five minutes.

These four rabbis were by now familiar to us; we knew all their quirks and characteristics. There were others who came to Schary Manor, but Brodsky, Hoffman, Silberfeld and Foster were the names we heard most often in answer to the question, "Who's the Rabbi?" One day, however, we heard a new name— Lewis Browne.

Rabbi Lewis Browne was young and handsome and his dress was unique. He wore long pointed collars and wide flowing ties, his coats were cut in the manner we believed to be "English style," and he had a small clipped mustache and spoke in a cultured accent that some people said was Harvard and others said was English. Each lady he met was charmed by the way he lifted her hand to his lips. He charmed the men too, for he was learned without being professorial, and he had a fund of funny stories that were manly without being vulgar.

Rabbi Browne hit Newark like a fresh spring rain. The Jewish prophets of the town spoke and ordained that he was going to be the most popular rabbi in town. His congregation was a new one called the Free Synagogue. To Mother this name had a clinical sound, and while she liked Rabbi Browne she couldn't understand why there was no Hebrew identification. The members of the congregation were reform Jews who had reformed even further than the members of the B'Nai Jeshurun, and most of them were politically liberal German Jews. They had no building of their own and had been conducting services in various halls which they had rented for their Friday night services, but when they retained Rabbi Browne as their shepherd they came to Schary Manor to request the use of our largest banquet room as a regular site for their services until the building drive for their own elaborately planned temple was completed.

Since we were a kosher establishment and never catered on Friday night, the banquet hall was always available, and Father thought that this would be a profitable arrangement which served a worthy purpose at the same time. But Zaida hated the idea. He maintained that the Free Synagogue was more a discussion group than a temple, and he thought their proceedings were sacrilegious. Mother acted as arbiter, but she was hardly objective, for she and Lillian and Frances had all fallen for Rabbi Browne's charm and intelligence. So the arrangement was made.

To me Lewis Browne was an extraordinary figure. Before we met he had heard from Mother that I had dreams about being a writer. Because he was a writer, he spoke to me with understanding and as one equal to another; he told me that it was a lonely business but one that could not be denied. Writing too was a religion, he said. I was so impressed that I started wearing long collars and wide ties like Rabbi Browne, but Lil teased me so unmercifully that I stopped wearing them.

Zaida regretted Mother's decision, but he didn't fight it. On Friday nights he would have an early dinner and leave the house to walk to the Anshe Russia temple before the sun set. After services there were always discussions and debates at the *shul* so Zaida knew he would not be home until long after the members of the Free Synagogue had gone. They arrived after dinner to begin their observances at eight, and would be out of the hall by nine forty-five.

The Free Synagogue lasted in Schary Manor only a few short weeks. What broke up the harmony and unity of the congregation was Rabbi Browne's second lecture, whose title was "The Life of Jesus." Even the most sophisticated of the congregants weren't ready for that. As Rabbi Browne started his surprise sermon there was a hushed but indignant murmur. A few of the congregation got up and walked out politely but hurriedly. The next interruption was neither polite nor hurried. A man rose and called out, "This is not the place for such a discussion. It's a disgrace in a temple. Either you stop or I resign as vice-president."

Lewis Browne didn't stop, and the Free Synagogue lost a vice-president, who took with him his wife and daughter and son-in-law. Lil and I, witnesses to the debacle, had mixed reactions. I was sorry that Browne was getting into hot water, but I agreed that he had put himself there. Lil tried to be open-minded, but she was worried about what Zaida would have to say.

Recognizing that he was on a sticky wicket, Rabbi Browne tried to turn the tide by talking of understanding. He said that fear was ignorance, that he was talking about a famous and important Jew as a man, not as the Messiah. But the more he talked the clearer it became that his support was dwindling. Finally he came to an abrupt end and the service was concluded.

One or two people congratulated him, but the rest filed out, silent until they reached the front hall. Then, feeling free to express their doubts, loud and passionate arguments erupted. The ex-vice-president, who was lying in wait outside Schary Manor, picked up where he had left off, and two calmer gentlemen had to restrain him from hitting one of the rabbi's supporters.

Understandably, Rabbi Browne was shaken by the experience. He declined Mother's offer of a cup of tea, but Mother promptly asked him to have dinner with us the following Friday night and he accepted. After he had gone, Mother told us that it would be best not to tell Zaida about the subject of the sermon. We all agreed that it was a discreet suggestion.

When Pa came home from his Friday-night pinochle game at Uncle Mike's, he thought it was a great joke. While he liked Lewis Browne, he had said before, "He talks like a rabbi but looks like a floorwalker. He won't be around by next Rosh ha-Shanah."

When Zaida arrived, we all greeted him extravagantly to prevent him from suspecting anything. I always watched for him and opened the door, because on the Sabbath he never carried a key and would not even press the doorbell. The Sabbath was a day of rest, and for Zaida everything rested, including kilowatt power. Normally I would tease him and keep him waiting for an extra few minutes outside the door. He would wait patiently, and when I would let him in he would say merely, *"Chochem."* But tonight I had the door open when he got to the steps and called out, "Good *Shabbas."* Unfortunately the Anshe Russia was not an island, and in the mysterious way of town gossip, which flies faster than light, word had already reached Zaida as he strolled home. He had met some friends who had been at Oheb Sholem, who had met some friends who had been at B'Nai Abraham, who had met some friends who had been at the Free Synagogue. The Jewish community was buzzing with the startling news of Rabbi Browne's sermon on the life of Jesus.

Zaida's first angry comment was, *"Ich hub dir gezogt"* (I told you so). He felt that Schary Manor had been disgraced and that he had been dishonored. Perhaps it was time for him to go to the Home for the Aged, he said. In a Jewish family this was as desperate a statement as, "I think I'll kill myself." While Jewish communities have always sponsored and built homes for the aged, families try to avoid sending their kin to these institutions; usually they are reserved for the old and infirm who have no close relatives to take care of them.

For my grandfather to have gone to a home for the aged would be as final and as disgraceful as committing suicide.

But hot tea and jam and sponge cake calmed Zaida down a little, and he went to bed, reluctantly agreeing not to move out for the time being. But never, no, never, would he set eyes on Rabbi Browne. This presented a problem for Mother, who remembered her invitation to Browne for dinner the next Friday night. It was solved the next day by Lewis Browne himself, who knew Zaida; he called Mother and said he thought it would be an embarrassment for him to come. Mother reluctantly agreed.

There was a sharp drop in members at the Free Synagogue's convocation on the following Friday night. Though some new curious souls dropped by to take in Browne's next bombshell, the total figure was less. There was no bombshell; Browne, perhaps with studied appropriateness, spoke on the Book of Job. On the following Friday the number in attendance was even smaller. In a few short weeks the Free Synagogue as then constituted disappeared, and Lewis Browne departed from town, leaving a mixed but imperishable memory in the minds of many Newarkers.

We did not hear of Lewis Browne again until he wrote his first best seller, *How Odd of God*. Then everybody heard his name.

18

Chicken under Glass

There were times during the years we were in the catering business when even my mother's indomitable patience was tried to the breaking point—but only up to the point. Never did she indulge in a tantrum. Under extraordinary stress, she would turn red, clamp her lips together to fight back tears of frustration or aggravation, and clutch her hands while she wordlessly counted as many numbers as necessary to collect her thoughts. Then she would make a sweeping gesture and say, "*Schwimm darüber,*" a colloquial German phrase meaning "Swim over it."

Mother's resourcefulness was demonstrated on the day we catered a lunch at the Y.M.H.A. for the Jewish Women's Council. The first course was a pineapple delight, a fancy name that Pa had made up for fruit salad served in scooped pineapple shells. Both the pineapples and the fruit salad were prepared at the Manor, and when we arrived at the Y.M.H.A. Sidney and I set up the two hundred and fifty shells in military precision on serving tables placed off the main auditorium. Then we went down to the kitchen to bring up the fruit salad. There Mother was supervising the heating of the chickens and potatoes and clear consommé, and she came back upstairs with us to see whether we really had enough fruit. But in the pantry where the shells had been arranged there was nothing but empty tables; the two hundred and fifty shells that had been there only ten minutes before had disappeared.

A frantic search produced the horrible news that two of the Y janitors had come into the serving pantry, and seeing what were to them obviously useless pineapple shells, had swept them into garbage cans and taken them down to the cellar. We made our way downstairs, took one look, and knew there was no way of salvaging the pineapple, now decorated with dirt, cigarette butts and ashes. The janitors were eager to make up for their error; they suggested high-pressure water hoses and brushes. Mother thanked them but refused, comforted the two men, and led us back to the kitchen. Tight-lipped, red-faced and clutching her hands, she kept muttering, "*Nu, schwimm darüber.*"

It was eleven-thirty. The guests were to eat at twelve-thirty. Mother told me to go to Schillings' grocery store on College Place. It was too late to think of preparing pineapple scoops, even if by some miracle Schillings' had a hundred and twenty-five pineapples on hand. I was to get grapefruit. Sidney and I jumped into the truck, found the necessary fruit, and returned within twenty minutes. Mother, Sidney, Fleischer, Rosie and I went to work halving grapefruit, scooping them, scalloping the edges and filling them with salad. The final touches included a maraschino cherry, a dash of ginger ale and the placing of two tiny flags, one Old Glory, the other the Star of David. From that time on, whenever we catered a dinner or luncheon outside of the Manor, there was a standing order never to leave the pineapple shells unattended.

On a number of occasions, affairs at Schary Manor were cancelled because of sudden illness or, sometimes, death. Of course the food was always paid for by the unhappy sponsors, and Mother would ship it out to the Orphan Asylum, the Home for the Aged or to the various hospitals. In one instance the groom was arrested for bootlegging on the morning of his wedding, but the revenue agents, showing touching sentiment, helped delay the police proceedings so that the ceremony could be performed and the dinner served. The police on watch were guests of the bride's family. The new bridegroom served only a short term and came home to a happy married life.

Then there was the wedding between the daughter of a man who headed one bootlegging syndicate and the son of the head of a rival syndicate. It was an extravagant affair. The gentlemen were all in white tie and holster, the ladies in tulle and sequins. The liquor was supplied by both families and there was a huge amount of it. While no one expected trouble, both sides took no chances. Sober gentlemen stood in appointed places, keeping an eye on their opposite numbers, who they knew to be as well armed and as competent as themselves.

The party progressed from the polite and sedate

atmosphere of the ceremony to the joyous camaraderie of the dinner, to boisterousness afterward, and finally into abandon. One of the drunken guests started the real fun. He grabbed a friend's coattails and ripped them smartly up the middle. It provided a good laugh, somebody did it to someone else, and in a few minutes every tail coat was torn asunder. The sober gunsels were all dressed in tuxedo and didn't get into the act.

Mother and Father watched the goings-on with some alarm. A free-for-all shooting match in Schary Manor was certainly not an advertisement for future business. But as the evening waned and guests left in black limousines, we began to breathe a bit easier. Unfortunately the two chiefs and their menacing staff of gunmen stayed on and on, and as they began to sober up, there were traces of growing discord. Since it was almost dawn, Mother thought that it would be a good idea to serve the remaining guests a "light breakfast" of bread, eggs, cheese, sturgeon, lox, tomatoes, sour cream, whitefish and coffee. They ate themselves out of the headachy bitterness of a hangover into the comfortable stupor of overfed children, and left at last without a shot having been fired or a fist lifted.

The waiters—and even I—all got hundred-dollar bills for our services. Added to the five- and ten-dollar tips I had been getting all evening, this made me feel that I'd never be poor again. But both parties to the wedding were so pleased that they insisted on doing something more for Mother and Father. They had paid for the wedding in cash, and a handsome sum it was, but now in the early light of morning they wanted to do something extra—anything. Mother suggested that it

would be nice if they gave some money to the Home
for the Aged and the Orphan Asylum.

"How much?" asked the bride's father.

"Whatever you think is right. Whatever you can afford," said Mother.

"Well, I can afford anything. What's right?" he insisted.

Father was tired and irritable. "Maybe a thousand
dollars," he said.

"Peanuts," said the groom's father. "I'll send them
each five G's."

"Okay by me," said the bride's father. "I'll do the
same."

The next day both the Home and the Asylum were
ten thousand dollars richer.

Afterward Mother said she didn't want to cater any
more affairs for bootleggers, but Pa pointed out that
there were so many of them it hardly seemed sensible
to cross them off the list.

Another crisis was the wedding supper which was
almost ruined by a new pantry assistant who put salt
in the sugar bowls. Luckily the mistake was discovered
before most of the guests had salted their fruit cups.
But perhaps Mother's most difficult moment as a caterer
was the morning she was faced with chicken under
glass.

It came about this way. The pantry tables where
Mother prepared her spring chickens for roasting ran
parallel to our driveway, and above them was a row of
refectory windows. One Sunday morning Mother was
working with Fleischer on three hundred portions of
chicken, which had been obtained by splitting in half

one hundred and fifty young springers. Mother had a special recipe for stuffing chickens; it was more a paste than a stuffing, and she would carefully insert it between the skin and the flesh of the breast of each halved chicken. It was a delicate operation, but Mother was expert at it, and when done the stuffing seemed like part of the chicken. It was a specialty of Schary Manor.

On this particular morning the chicken halves were on the pantry boards and Mother was just beginning work when there was a crash of breaking glass and two of the refectory panes showered down on the chickens. John, our head porter, had been shoveling snow to clear a path from the driveway when his shovel had slipped and smashed into the glass.

I was in the kitchen eating breakfast, and at the sound I rushed to the pantry to find Mother in her characteristic pose of forced patience moaning softly at the tableau of destruction. The chickens, heavily sprinkled with glass, represented the main course for three hundred guests that night.

Outside, John, looking at the fruit of his labors, was repeating endlessly, "Sonamonbitch." Nobody else said anything; all of us stood silently and looked at the mess while Mother pursed her lips and clutched her hands. Finally she turned and faced us. "It's Sunday, so we can't get a hundred and fifty springers. Even if we could, we couldn't get them cleaned and koshered and cooked in time."

"Belle," said Pa, "don't worry. I'll go to Prince Street and find some capons, turkeys, anything. It's an accident. What can we do?"

"No," said Mother decisively. "Fleischer, get me some pails of water."

She decided to wash the chickens. This decision was her responsibility, and she refused to let anyone help. Father protested, but Mother was firm. When the pails were ready we all stood by for instructions. Mother permitted us to pick up any glass that wasn't touching the fowl on the table. Then she took the first half, shook it, peered at it, finally put it in the water and cleaned it carefully, searching all the while with her eyes and fingers for any speck of glass. As she worked she gave instructions to Fleischer to proceed with the stuffing of the birds. He was a little clumsy, but Lil was almost as good as Mother at the job and she chipped in to help.

After Mother had cleaned the first twenty or thirty pieces, she slowly drained the water off and looked in the bottom of the pail. When she found some glass which had sunk to the bottom she was relieved; the plan was working.

Morning fled into noon, then afternoon into dusk, before the work was done. Every chicken had been washed and cleaned, the stuffing was completed, and the roasting begun. Mother went upstairs. She had cut her fingers in a few places and her hands were covered with pieces of plaster; she was tired and afraid. But she had done the best she could. Zaida, Pa, Lil and I talked to her before she took a short nap. She asked each of us to pray a long prayer that all would be well.

When the guests filed in for the wedding, all of us gave them a gay and proper welcome, but we were scarcely breathing. At the end of the ceremony when, following tradition, the groom broke the wine glass under foot, we all shuddered. Then the supper began.

The fruit cup.

The gefilte fish and horseradish and aspic.

The noodle soup.

The sherbet.

And then the roast chickens, served with peas and carrots in potato ramekins. They looked delicious, but any one of them could mean a torn stomach.

No one collapsed during dinner.

The speeches and the dances went on until three o'clock in the morning, until Ralph Reichenthal and Jerry Norton and their orchestra played "Goodnight, Sweetheart." We didn't sit around in the kitchen afterward; none of us was hungry. We all went to bed troubled and uneasy.

The next day Mother got a call from the bride's mother thanking her for the wonderful wedding and the magnificent food—particularly the roast chicken.

"Did everybody like it?" asked Mother.

"Everybody," said the happy lady.

After two or three days of glorious "no-news-is-good-news," Dr. Nash, who was visiting one of our boarders abed with a cold, was cross-examined by Mother. As casually as possible she said, "If, for instance, anybody ate a small piece of glass, how long would it take to find out it was hurting him?"

"Did you eat glass?"

"Well, maybe there was a piece in something I ate," said Mother.

"When?" asked Dr. Nash.

"Oh, last Sunday maybe."

"Forget it," said the doctor. "If you haven't got any pain or any bleeding, it didn't do you any harm—but I don't recommend it as part of the regular menu."

We all laughed so loud and long at this comment that Dr. Nash looked startled.

After a week we felt that all must be well. Then Mother got another call from the bride's mother. "My daughter just got back from the honeymoon and she wanted me to call you and tell you something. She said that all her life she would never forget the lovely wedding you catered, and she'll never forget the marvelous dinner."

"That's so nice of her," said my mother.

"One little thing?"

"Yes?"

"She asked if sometime she maybe could come over and see how you make those wonderful roast chickens."

"Any time, darling, tell her any time," said Mother.

"Believe me," said the bride's mother, "it's an occasion I'll never forget."

"Thank you," said Ma, and when she hung up she added, "And neither will I."

Some months later, when we were asked by a customer if we ever included chicken under glass in any of our menus, Mother said that she had had experience with the dish and would be delighted to accommodate the lady.

19

The Wisteria Room Meets N.Y.U.

Father always wanted me to be a lawyer. To him a parchment diploma written in Latin, framed and hanging on the wall, was solid, secure and respectable. When it was clear that I would never make a lawyer, he settled for my being a businessman. This too meant "security"; what he really meant by that, of course, was respectability.

As I have said earlier, Pa loathed show business; it was a business for tramps, just as writing was a business for bums. He would "prove" his case by talking about the Gottliebs' daughter, whose stage name had been Lorraine Lovelace. She had last been heard of in New Orleans, where she had married a haberdasher. As everybody knew, New Orleans was a sinkhole of sin.

Another example was Frederick Kaplan, Adolph Kaplan's boy, who went to college for four years and then tried to become a writer on a newspaper in Milwaukee. He had ended up doing publicity for a circus and was disinherited.

Oddly enough Pa didn't feel this way about artists. He admired sculptors and painters. My cousin, Saul Schary, the son of Pa's brother Rudolph, was his favorite nephew, and when Saul developed into a fine painter my father was proud. Art was something you could look at, touch and enjoy; it was a special gift, and Saul was always a welcome and honored guest. But the theatre and writing were not *art*. Since my ambitions at seventeen were to write for the theatre Father regarded this as a compound tragedy, and he used every conceivable device to make me behave like a businessman.

Our catering establishment was so well booked and Father's imagination was so expansive that we grew too large for the four-story house at 604 High Street, and Father bought a great auditorium in Newark which had a main ballroom accommodating two thousand people. (It also had the biggest kitchen in New Jersey.) It was a cavernous structure, all red brick on the outside and wood and plaster inside, and it had a permanent smell of beer from the bar, cooking from the three kitchens, disinfectant from the battery of rest rooms, and an odor of paint because something was always being painted. (Father was always thinking of a new color to try on the walls.)

Father loved the auditorium; it made him feel substantial. He could walk for hours through the long tunnels that honeycombed the cellar, up the many staircases that led to the upper floors, into the balcony that surrounded the main ballroom, and down the grand stairway that was made of marble. We knew that he loved the place because he would speak German as he marched around, and he only spoke German when he was feeling expansive.

There was a great deal of redecorating to do when we took over the auditorium, and Father was busy for weeks with decorators, designers and painters. Old Man Brown, the boss painter, had a heavy, rattling cough which punctuated his growled words, and a Hassan cigarette always drooped from his lips. It was wet a third of the way down, and the smoke curled into his eyes and gave him a perpetual squint. For years he listened, mixed paint, slapped it on the wall, and coughed and smoked his way through the auditorium and its innumerable color combinations. During the time we ran the place there was never a day when Mr. Brown or some of his men were not at work. Mr. Brown hated Father's color schemes, but the employment was steady and the food was delicious.

Father had one favorite room which was completely his conception. The Wisteria Room was a sprawling banquet hall on the first floor that looked out on the only piece of lawn on Belmont Avenue. At the end of the lawn was a six-foot-high wood fence that hid the pavement. Papa loved to stand in one of the three doorways that opened on the lawn and stare out at the grass and flowers. He always hummed a German song when he did this.

The Wisteria Room was designed to look like a German beer garden. The walls were papered with cloud murals; pasted over these were simulated wooden posts, cutouts from another pattern, which formed an arbor effect. Dangling from the walls were bunches of paper wisteria. The tables were covered with red and white checkered cloths. The gilded café chairs had rattan seats. On the walls were shelves lined with German pewter and porcelain beer steins, but beer was served in huge glasses—never from the steins on the shelves.

As soon as it was finished, the Wisteria Room became popular, and all of the banquets served in it were supervised by Pa himself. Our head waiter, Frank, was shunted off to some other room on these occasions. Pa would watch the service and the conduct of the guests from his favorite perch near the newly painted fire hose that hung in a niche appropriately covered by paper wisteria.

From the foregoing, it can be gathered that it was a certain evidence—and test—of his faith in my future as a businessman when Pa decided to place the N.Y.U. freshman dinner I had arranged in the Wisteria Room. A few weeks earlier I had gone to a high-school fraternity banquet in the Pennsylvania Hotel in New York, and some of my "brothers" wanted to know if they could book their college freshman dinner at our place in Newark. They explained that it would be nicer and more of a lark for their classmates. I discussed a menu with them and wrote out a simple contract for one hundred guests and a receipt for the fifty-dollar deposit they gave me to insure the date. I made a copy of the agreement for myself, they signed it, and the next morning Pa was delighted when I showed the papers to him. I had selected the right menu at the right price and the deposit was signal proof of my skill. As a reward he told me that the dinner would be held in the Wisteria Room.

That morning Pa asked me to make the rounds of the building with him. As we walked up and down and through the structure he bellowed his orders: Mr. Brown, currently occupied in the corridor leading to the bar downstairs, was to paint the large checkroom on the second floor as the next assignment; the janitors were to clean the stage, where confetti still lingered from a show staged two nights before; Frank Monahan was to place tables closer to the platform in the lower ballroom and get some new waiters from the union, since it appeared that the older ones had an ingenious racket with the bartender to bilk the management; Fleischer, Mother's chief cook, was to ask the chicken dealer to deliver the chickens earlier than usual in the morning. (Fleischer told my father to mind his own business; he knew exactly when the chickens should be delivered. Fleischer was a little man made of springs, with a loud voice and a short temper. He also had Father's number, and while he adored my mother, he would rip off his apron and threaten to quit if Father came into the kitchen during the serving of a banquet. I don't know whether Father was afraid he might kill Fleischer if he ever hit him or whether he liked him; at any rate, Fleischer stayed on. Whatever, Father's deafness in his right ear came in handy now, and we walked by without another word and continued on our rounds.)

After an hour's inspection we returned to the office and my father ordered near beer for both of us. He had never done this before. We sat and drank together and he looked at me and smiled happily. Papa told me that he knew the college affair would be a nice one and that he expected me to work the Wisteria Room with him on the night of the dinner. Then he began talking about a chain of kosher catering places that would cover the country. Suddenly the thought of being a successful caterer seemed to me a good idea and highly rewarding.

On the night of the dinner I dressed in a dark business suit and checked over all the arrangements in the Wisteria Room. There was a corps of waiters and the room looked bright in the spring dusk. The place really did resemble a German beer garden. I told Sidney, our chief pantryman, who was to function as the captain, that the grapefruit was to be on the table before dinner started. As usual, little American flags were stuck in the grapefruit halves. This was one of my father's touches; he believed that every happy occasion was an opportunity to remind us all of what a great country we lived in. (This despite the fact that at that time we had a Republican administration; to my father it was only a demonstration of how enduring we were. We could even put up with Coolidge, he argued, with no great loss to the American system.)

The collegians were due to arrive at seven. At six o'clock some freshmen arrived with two prisoners (that's how they were identified—as prisoners). They explained to us that each year the sophomores tried to learn where the freshman dinner was being held. In answer to my father's "Why?" they explained vaguely that it was all "traditional," but that anyhow the sophomores wouldn't find out this year because their two "spies" had been captured.

The episode seemed silly to Papa, but as a fellow fraternity member, I persuaded him to let the freshmen lock up the prisoners in one of the rooms in the cellar.

Papa agreed, on condition that "the spies" got something to eat. He liked these college boys, he said. "Maybe you could go to N.Y.U. and get a diploma?"

"Maybe," I said.

"Believe me, a college man you can respect. He has dignity, style—like a gentleman." So saying, he examined me, straightened my tie, and told me I needed a haircut.

At 7:06 P.M. the Wisteria Room was full of N.Y.U. freshmen standing in front of their seats, eight to each table, when suddenly there was a babble of sound from behind the wooden fence that faced the Wisteria Room. I heard a roar of motors and saw the tops of two large trucks come to a halt. Then there were yells and screams, and over the fence figures appeared and began dropping onto the lawn—first five, then ten, then scores. The sophomores had arrived. As I watched in horror, both sides girded for battle. As the sophomores charged, Father, aroused by the sounds and by the frantic shouts of Sidney, appeared in the room. As the invaders piled in they were met by an opening barrage of grapefruit hurled by the freshmen.

Father bellowed for everybody to stop—"Gentlemen, gentlemen, please"—but the uproar swallowed his voice. There was nothing to say, but much to do. These nice collegians were messing up Father's beloved Wisteria Room, and he went into action. He plunged in, flinging freshmen and sophomores indiscriminately to the floor. The room was a brawling, shapeless, motley mess. I moved to Father's side and felt a fist hit my cheek; in retaliation I swung out and hit someone. Father was roaring English, Yiddish, Polish and German oaths and tossing young bodies right and left. Hands ripped at our clothes, and slaps and punches stung our bodies. Finally Father stomped his way through the struggling mass to the fire hose. As I followed he grabbed the nozzle and yelled at me to turn on the water. When I twisted the ring the force of the water almost yanked the nozzle from Father's hands, but he held on and directed the powerful spray at the gladiators. Freshmen and sophomores alike were sloshed out of the Wisteria Room in common wet misery. A few daring ones who tried to reach the hose were swept down and out or were slugged by Sidney.

At 7:14 P.M. the Wisteria Room was empty—and a shambles. There was loud yelling and laughing outside, the sound of trucks departing, and then only the cluck-cluck of Sidney's tongue as he viewed the damage, and the drip-drip of the water as it fell from overturned tables and chairs. The wreckage was complete. Half grapefruits stuck to the walls; steins were broken or missing; the paper wisteria hung in dismal clumps.

Shuddering, I dared not speak or move from Father's side. I had felt the fury of his temper before, and as I waited for him to turn on me, I had mixed feelings of resentment, resignation and apprehension. For it had dawned on me that I had written everything into the contract but the damage clause.

I waited for Father to turn and look at me. The only sounds were of his heavy breathing and the drip-drip of the water. Finally Father spun around, stared at me and placed one big palm against my chest. "Businessman," he said in a quiet voice, and pushed me gently aside. He walked out of the room.

Sidney and I and the porters stayed to clean up. Two hours later I remembered the prisoners in the locker downstairs. The door was open and they had gone. Papa was waiting for me at the top of the cellar stairs. He told me that he had sent them away. "Bummers," he said. "They didn't even have carfare. I gave them two dollars. I don't want you to go to N.Y.U.— never."

We wandered into the Wisteria Room, now cleaned but still damp. "Tomorrow," Father said, "I got to get Brown to get the painters in here." I nodded meekly and followed him back to the office and listened as he called my mother at Schary Manor, where she was in charge of a large wedding party.

"Belle, how's the wedding? Good. Here? Nothing. Your son I hope should be a good writer, because believe me a businessman he's not."

When he hung up, Pa said, "Go get some beer. And tomorrow, a haircut."

20

Happy New Year

As it is for everyone who works in the catering or restaurant business, New Year's Eve was always a busy night for us. None of us ever enjoyed the usual holidays in the conventional manner. On New Year's Eve, Decoration Day, the Fourth of July, Labor Day, Thanksgiving, Christmas, and all Saturday nights, we were always working. We all became night people the day my parents went into catering.

This played havoc with my high school attendance, and Mother or Father had to make frequent trips to school to explain why I missed so many morning classes. Their excuses were listened to patiently by Principal William Wiener of Central High School, who then would explain why it was impossible for him to make allowances or to change class schedules to suit the peculiar hours of our business. As a result, I was suspended many times, which distressed Father greatly. At this point he still had his heart set on my becoming a lawyer, and he knew that before I could get into law school I had to have a high school diploma. For a few weeks after each warning I would manage to get up in time for morning assembly and all would go well; then, over-tired, I would come down with a cold or a fever, miss classes, go back to work, forget the morning alarm and the cycle would resume. Altogether, I left or was dismissed from high school on six different occasions, and though I kept going back, I never did get my diploma from Central High.

It wasn't until I was nineteen that I received a special dispensation from the Board of Education, which figured that at my advanced age I ought to be able to tackle a program that allowed me to go to both day and night school for three terms a year. Aided by many willing teachers, particularly Benjamin J. Stolper and Michael Conovitz, who helped me conquer my embarrassment by making me feel extraordinary instead of simple-minded, and who stimulated me constantly, I was able to get enough credits to make me eligible for law school.

But having achieved this goal, I went no further, because by then Pa realized that I was headed for show business. Nevertheless I worked harder than ever before in Schary Manor to try to prove to him that while he had lost a lawyer he had gained a waiter, chauffeur, hat-check boy, pantryman and dishwasher.

By now my brother Sam was in California seeking fame and fortune, first by dancing in ballrooms, then by singing over the radio. When these proved to be dead ends, he resumed his salesman's job. By then he and his first wife, Elsie, had gotten a divorce. In those days a divorce in a Jewish family was not taken lightly, and while we were not overly fond of Elsie, we were a little ashamed that Sam had broken off the alliance. Also, by this time Frances was married to Lou Freeman and Lil to Henry Waldman, an accountant from New York who was studying law. Pa was ecstatic; the family was taking on stature.

Helped by an incredible staff of workers, whom Mother always seemed able to corral, my parents and I put in long hours. On busy nights Frances and Lil would help out and keep a family eye on the proceedings. One such night was New Year's Eve, 1924.

On that night there were two large banquets at Schary Manor, one a silver wedding anniversary for the Levys, the other a fiftieth birthday for a Mr. Schoen. In addition, the big auditorium we owned on Belmont Avenue had been converted into a restaurant, to which we invited people to celebrate for twenty dollars a couple. Though the upstairs ballroom had been rented to an Italian social club that paid us a flat fee for the use of the hall, we had to assign some members of the staff to run the near-beer bar and short-order restaurant. We had also agreed to cater a large banquet for a Jewish club in the armory at Plainfield, and our last commitment was to supply food for a small dinner party of forty people in Elizabeth, New Jersey.

In all, Mother and her chefs had to cook food for over two thousand people. The fruit salad was prepared in massive cauldrons; the soup was an ocean filled with noodles; fish dealers on Prince Street never had it so good; the chicken population of New Jersey was decimated by our kosher butchers; and pastries and kettles of coffee crowded every nook and cranny.

Frank Monahan and Sidney were in charge of signing up as many union waiters as they could persuade to enlist. The recruiting had begun weeks before. When we ran out of regular union waiters, we enlisted help from private homes; butlers, maids and cooks who had the night off got special bonuses for working for us that New Year's Eve.

There had to be a master plan of operations for such an evening. Each party had to have a maitre d' representing the management. Mother was in command of logistics, and her post was Schary Manor, the home base, from which she could supervise the movement of supplies. Lil, Frances and Sidney Rapp were to stay with her to handle the two banquets at the Manor.

Father's assignment was the auditorium. With him was our head chef, Fleischer, who was temperamental but efficient, and would brook no nonsense from Father. Also, because of the big social goings-on upstairs, Father was in charge of a detail of special police officers who patrolled the place to make certain that there were no violations of the Volstead Act. Pa took the law seriously; if he spotted anyone pouring alien liquid into the near-beer he would usher the offender outside. If he didn't choose to be ushered, he'd be dragged out by force— and unconscious, if Father lost his temper.

The small party in Elizabeth was to be chaperoned by Greenberg, one of Fleischer's top assistants, with a suitable number of waiters and helpers, guided by Lou, Frances' husband, who was happy to lend a hand for the evening.

That left Plainfield—and Frank Monahan, assisted by me, was in charge of that huge assembly. The chef in charge was Rabinowitz, Fleischer's second in command.

Early in the morning I drove our truck to Elizabeth to deliver the dishes, napery, silver and "basics" (salt, pepper, bread, celery, olives, lettuce). In the meantime two trucks rented from the Amsterdam Brothers were delivering the same cargo to Plainfield.

As the day passed, the tempo of activity increased. Merchants kept arriving with fruit and vegetables. Bakers, smelling of fresh-baked dough, delivered hundreds of loaves of bread and rolls. Chicken dealers brought extra birds to be plucked and singed and cleaned. There was enough fish to stock a large lake. Everywhere I went there were shouts and commands and questions and curses. "When's the truck going to Elizabeth?" "Get busy. The people in Plainfield eat at nine o'clock." "Did anybody hear from the ice people?" "Damn it, I cut my finger." "If that's a good chicken, my name is Moishe the Royta." "My God, we forgot the olives." And above all this, John, driving himself and his porters mercilessly, could be heard with his comment, "Sonamonbitch."

Through it all moved Zaida, observing and not giving an inch, despite the chaos, to any dietary violation. Whether two people or two thousand, everything had to be kosher.

Schary Manor was thick with steam and the odor of singed chicken, freshly sliced fruit, soup and boiling fish. It was cold outdoors, but we all sweated as if it were July. I was on the move all day with the truck—to Elizabeth, to stores, to Plainfield, to and from the auditorium—transporting people and supplies.

As we took a ten-minute break at four o'clock for a quick snack, Mother said, "If Bubeh were still alive, she'd call all of us crazy."

In Plainfield, Frank called in additional items to be packed for my final run. As each item was added, my hysterical feeling grew that I'd never get the truck to move an inch. By five-thirty the noise and excitement were unendurable, but endured they were—except by one of John's helpers, who had been secretly nipping at a flask. When sufficiently drunk, he took umbrage at something Sidney said, grabbed a knife and ran at him. Sidney side-stepped, tripped him, grabbed the knife, clipped him once and threw him into the back yard to sober up.

By six-thirty I was on my final trip to Plainfield. I felt ridiculous. I was dressed in a new tuxedo, freshly shaved, smelling like a gigolo, with my hair soaked with *eau de quinine*, and driving a groaning Chevrolet truck with kettles sloshing, dishes rattling and John beside me dozing to get some renewed strength for the rigors ahead. I felt alone. Why, just this once, couldn't I go out with Hetzie Makowsky or Ira Kahn or Saul Glucksman on one of their heavy dates? I realized that I couldn't remember ever going out even on a Saturday night, and I felt very sorry for myself. Here I was, nattily dressed, with nowhere to go except a kosher dinner in Plainfield.

It began to snow. "That's all we need," I said aloud, "a blizzard." Talking in his sleep, John answered suitably. "Sonamonbitch," he muttered.

When we reached the armory in Plainfield, it was a madhouse. Frank and the waiters were setting up tables; Rabinowitz was heating food and shouting at his people; florists and flag hangers were still decorating the hall. I took one look and knew we'd never make it. Ever the pragmatist, Frank suggested that I take off my coat and start moving my rear end. By nine-thirty, only half an hour late, we were standing in an elegant hall. Each place setting had its paper hat, noisemaker, streamers, confetti and the required knives, forks, glasses and napkin roll.

The dinner began. The music was loud and brassy, the service was excellent, and the hours sped away. It seemed only a few minutes before the orchestra was playing "Auld Lang Syne." But there was no mistletoe and no one to kiss except Frank, Rabinowitz and John. Gravely, we all shook hands. Then I tried to call Mother at Schary Manor, but after an endless wait for the operator, our phone proved to be busy. I went back to work.

We began clearing the tables by one-thirty. Luckily the Plainfield burghers were not night owls; by two o'clock even the last stubborn drunks were gone and the band had played "Goodnight, Sweetheart." The Amsterdam movers and John and the waiters were already loading the trucks. At last the lights were dimmed and the armory assumed the look of a tired old harridan who had had a grand evening but had collapsed the moment the guests left. By three o'clock I was driving Frank, John and myself home in the truck. Frank sang dirty songs to remind us that it was a joyous occasion and at four o'clock we pulled up to Schary Manor.

Lou had long since returned from Elizabeth with Greenberg. The two parties at the Manor had gone well and were just breaking up into little groups of tired, happy and overfed people. Mother, dressed in a beautiful dark-blue gown, looked as fresh as dew and was entertaining some of her friends with her funny Jewish stories. She kissed me and wished me a happy new year, then suggested I go to the auditorium and bring Father home.

When I got there the Italian social was all over, and Tom Sheridan, the chief of our special police, told me that it had been a quiet evening—no fights, no undue excitement. The porters were cleaning up the place and the musicians were leaving. There is nothing that looks lonelier than a group of musicians leaving a hall late at night carrying their black instrument cases. They appear to be undertakers who have just interred a good party.

Downstairs, our restaurant party was on its last legs. Father gave me a bear hug and asked how things had gone in Plainfield. I gave him a glowing report, putting special emphasis on my own good services, and he was pleased.

In a few minutes Jerry Norton's orchestra played its last song. Pa told Tom Sheridan to lock up and gave him a fifty-dollar bill as a bonus for a good night's work; then he and I got wearily into the Chevrolet to go home. Pa was tired but happy; it was the biggest night's business we had ever catered, and the gross receipts would come to almost thirty-five thousand dollars. He had no idea what profit that represented, but it would be a handsome one, and he told me that next Friday night he was going to take all of us out for a "high time."

At the Manor, Frances and Lou, Lil and Henry, Mother, Father, Zaida and I all gathered in the dim light of 6:00 A.M. We were white with fatigue, but there was a tableful of cheese and eggs and rye bread and hot milk and coffee to revive us. And there were stories to tell: about Mr. White (real name Weiss) who got drunk and put his hand on Sarah Fischberg's behind; about the Kridels, our boarders, who had been guests at one of the parties and who had gone to bed before twelve o'clock because they said they always wanted to be alone on New Year's Eve (Mother thought this very romantic); about George Furst, the lawyer, and his brother Tony, who had started a kissing waltz contest.

Mother told us about the hands she had noticed. This was one of Mother's great stunts; she would look at a man's hands and nine times out of ten could guess what business he was in. There was, she insisted, a special look about the hands of a butcher or a ladies' tailor or a baker or a banker. She was right so often that we used to tease her and say she must be cheating and only pretending to be guessing. Mother was also a good mimic, and she imitated some of the guests who tried to speak "high-tone" and then reverted to gutter accents when they had had a drink or two. Then she gave an impersonation of Mr. Ginsberg, who spoke like an ox, and of Mrs. Klein, who twittered like a bird.

When the first streaks of dawn came into the kitchen, Pa rose to make a toast with his cup of coffee. "Thank God," he said, "we are all here on this New Year, except, God bless him, our son Sam. May we all have good health and be happy together."

We all sang "Auld Lang Syne," except Zaida, who suggested we now sing "Hatikvah." We sang that too, and then Lou and Frances went home to their apartment, and the rest of us went upstairs to sleep. As I got into bed I wondered wistfully what Hetzie and Saul and Ira had done that night.

I slept until six o'clock the next evening, when I

had to get up to go to work in the checkroom. A party was being given that evening by Hadassah to open a drive for funds to be spent on a home for underprivileged children. I am ashamed to admit that it occurred to me that I was an excellent candidate.

21

Home Away
from Home

In the summer of 1925 I got a job as a camp counselor at Cedar Lake Camp on Lake Tiorati in the Catskills. It was the first time that I had been on my own for any length of time away from our warm family life, and I went to camp with a feeling of uneasiness.

Mr. Ezekial Londau, one of our boarders, who had always encouraged my literary yearnings and elevated my reading habits by guiding me to Anatole France, Stendhal and Joseph Conrad, was responsible for my new environment. He had suggested that work as a dramatic counselor in a summer camp would be good training.

Cedar Lake Camp was operated by the Y.M.H.A., and the youngsters came in two shifts of one hundred and fifty each in July and August. Some of the campers received scholarships—that is, they were hardship cases of tough boys from poor backgrounds who needed discipline. Most of the other campers were from middle-class New Jersey families.

Three of my friends worked at the camp: Harold Lasser, a hurdler at Michigan, was track and field counselor; Marvin Mostwill, from Rutgers, and Norman Levy of Princeton, a member of the college lacrosse team, worked as general counselors.

I had prepared for the summer's work by accumulating a pile of such simple one-act plays as *The Hand of Siva, A Night at the Inn* and *A Game of Chess*, as well as a variety of poems, speeches and quotations. I had also written a pageant for Fourth of July, a religious pageant about the Maccabees, and had made up a long list of songs, tricks and games.

But I had one serious problem. I had lied to Mr. Henry Mayer, who had hired me, when he asked me if I could swim. I had said yes, but the truth was I couldn't swim a stroke. My aquatic experience had been limited to jumping up and down in the surf at Bradley Beach, and the only time I had ever gone in over my head I had been yanked back to safety by an alert lifeguard. I didn't let my problem bother me, however. After all, there was an easy solution; all I had to do was swim.

The counselors arrived at Cedar Lake the week before the first group of campers. We swept cabins, set up beds, cleaned the grounds, cleared paths, washed down the kitchens, silverware and dishes, and were briefed on our general and individual duties. Within a few days I built a makeshift stage in the playhall, rigged up a curtain, devised spotlights out of strong flashlights, and built and painted some basic scenery flats for the summer's program.

Early each morning, again for an hour at midday, and finally at sunset, the staff went to the lake for a swim. There was a crib for the nonswimmers, but since it was built to accommodate young boys, it was only three feet deep. All the other counselors ignored the crib and plunged into the water from the diving board or the dock. For the first three days I said I was getting over a cold and had better not go into the water. I watched every move of my companions; I saw how they stroked the water, how they kicked their feet, how they jumped in and then came up for air. Of course I had seen people swim before, but the sport had never interested me. Now I *had* to be interested; every counselor was assigned to water patrol during swimming period, and if there was an emergency, it was obvious that I would have to do more than point and yell for help.

For three days I watched and I watched; then, alone, I would imitate the movements I'd seen. On the fourth day I told Walter Bossard, the swimming counselor, that I was going to try the water by getting into the crib. Since I was recovering from a cold, I explained, I had better get used to the icy lake water by degrees. He looked at me a little strangely, but said he thought it a fine idea. In I went to water that came up to my hips. Taking a deep breath, I flattened out in imitation of the dive I had seen the others make into the lake. But I landed flat on my stomach and knocked the wind out of my lungs. Popping to my feet, gasping for air, I looked over at Bossard, smiled knowingly and said, "Sure is cold." He nodded. Then I crouched down, slowly stretched my body—and began to swim. To my surprise, I moved, though my arms were flailing too fast and my head was under water. I held my breath for as long as I could, then popped up again and discovered I had gone about six feet.

Luckily the other counselors were swimming and diving and paying no attention to me—all except Walter Bossard. Strolling down to the crib, he said quietly with a gentleness I will never forget, "You can't swim."

It was a relief to confess. Walter told me to hang around after the others had gone back to camp; he said he would tell Mr. Mayer I was helping him caulk some of the boats. When the lake was deserted, he began to teach me how to swim.

By the time the boys arrived three days later, I could dive from the dock, swim fifty yards, and make a surface dive. However, though Walter Bossard was proud of his accomplishment, he was no fool, and for the first few weeks he assigned me to watch the non-swimmers splash around in the crib.

During the beginning of the season I was so busy and so excited by what I was doing that I thought little about my family. Sam was in California and I wrote him about my work, but the rest of the folks received only post cards and short notes. Lillian was away for the summer with her family; Frances and Lou and their son Joel were in Bradley Beach with Mother and Father, and I heard little from any of them. But every week or so Mother would send me a box of food, which was devoured by my colleagues after we had bedded down our charges at night, and I wrote her that her strudel and cake had made her the darling of Cedar Lake Camp.

My birthday is on August 31, and in 1925 I was

to be twenty years old. By then camp was almost over, and I was lonely. I had never been away from home for so long, and though I was almost a man, it was a special day and I was all alone. As dawn broke, my ten charges, known as "The Butchlets" (my nickname was "Butch" because I was tall, gaunt and ungainly), greeted me by singing "happy birthday." I was touched by their thoughtfulness, conveniently forgetting that I had casually mentioned my birthday the night before.

But the mail brought no greetings, and there was no phone call or message from Western Union. By early afternoon I was feeling sorry for myself; it was clear that I was out of sight and out of mind and that no loved one had been moved to mark this special birthday. I confided my misery to Harold Lasser. He provided no sympathy; his birthday, he reminded me, had been on August 1. He too had been twenty, and I hadn't bothered to congratulate him. I apologized, and congratulated him. He accepted my apology, and congratulated me. The exchange did nothing for either of us.

At three-thirty I was rehearsing Saturday night's show in the playhall when I was called to the telephone. It was Mother. She was calling from the other side of the lake; she had come up by train and bus and now was waiting for transportation to the camp.

The camp truck, our only vehicle in which to drive the four miles around the lake, was on an errand and would not be back until six o'clock. There was only one other way to get Mother—by boat. Mr. Mayer gave me permission to use a rowboat, and Harold Lasser, who loved my mother, volunteered to row across with me. The lake was about a mile and a half wide; the rowboat was low-flanked but seaworthy. Mother was waiting for us on the dock looking fresh as a flower. I hugged her. She was wearing her favorite dress, a lilac-colored print with a white lace collar, and was carrying a large, heavy box.

Suddenly I had some second thoughts. Mother was fifty-two, she had never swum a stroke, the lake was choppy, and the low gunwales of the boat always shipped water. I looked at her. "We'll manage," she said, telling me in two words that she knew what I was thinking—and to stop thinking.

We placed her in the stern, the box on her lap, and as we pulled oars she looked at us with a calm smile. I felt very grateful for her. She was beautiful and serene, and she had gone to such trouble on my birthday. I hated myself for having been such a self-pitying ninny and vowed that I would never forget this moment.

Harold and I rowed carefully, but we were all relieved when we reached the other side. Mother told us that it was the best ride she had ever had in a rowboat; of course it had been her first. Then I introduced her to Mr. Mayer, who offered her the use of his guest room. When we escorted her there, she suggested that we eat lightly at dinner; the box she had brought contained some surprises—enough for a dozen hungry young men, she said.

A few minutes later my sister Lillian called me from Long Island, and a telegram arrived from Frances. My family was still my family.

After dinner there was a campfire and we sang songs to the campers: "Ivan Petrofsky Skivar," "Blow the Man Down," and "There Were Three Jolly Fishermen." Then we told ghost stories, and when the boys were properly scared, we ushered them to bed and played taps.

Afterward the counselors convened to the playhall, where we opened the box. Inside was a feast. There was cold roast chicken, potato salad, pickles, rye bread, cold beef tongue, cole slaw, apple and cherry strudel, and cakes and tarts of all kinds. There were even napkins and a checkered tablecloth. Mr. Mayer, who had also been invited, proved a worthy guest by providing large pitchers of lemonade. Everybody sang "happy birthday," and we proceeded to gorge ourselves. It was after ten o'clock when all the food was gone. Mother had to catch a train at Tuxedo at eleven o'clock, and Mr. Mayer told me that I could use the camp truck to drive her there. This was equivalent to getting permission to use the presidential yacht.

The boys all thanked Mother, and we set off. It was the first time we had been alone since she had arrived. Mother opened her purse and brought out a package, a gift from Pa. It was a wrist watch, the first one I'd ever owned. We reached Tuxedo twenty minutes ahead of the train, and we sat and talked. I told Mother of the things I had learned during the summer; I even told her of a lesson I had learned that very day about selfishness—about my self-pity, my delight at seeing her and my realization that part of growing up was learning not to pamper oneself by expecting the small comforts of youth at the expense of others.

"Well, Sonny," Mother said, "it's like your telling me about how you learned to swim. You watched, you tried, then you got wet and lost your breath. It was no pleasure, but afterward it became a pleasure. It's like what a famous rabbi said: 'It is better in life if first you say "Oi," then afterward you learn to say "Ah." But if first you say "Ah," then have to say "Oi," it means you are making big mistakes.'"

When the train came in I kissed Ma goodbye and thanked her. We waved until the night separated us. By the time I got back to camp it was after midnight; it was September 1 and I was over twenty years old. As I settled into my blankets I sighed and said softly, "Ah."

22

Schary Manor Closes

In the fall of 1925 my parents sold their catering business. A year earlier we had built a new and glittering Schary Manor on Clinton Avenue, our third establishment, and into it Father had poured all his dreams. It was elegant, lush, and designed for convenience in catering. The Manor was famous in New Jersey for its food and service, and families came from Trenton, Plainfield, New Brunswick, the Oranges, Maplewood and Passaic. As the business prospered, Mother and Father acquired the luxuries that came with success. Father's clothes were more expensive and stylish, Mother's jewelry was more elaborate, and Lil and Frances, married to Henry and Lou, were the early beneficiaries of our prosperity.

My parents were comparatively young to think of retiring, but Father had invested in real estate which appeared to be increasing in value, and had decided that they had worked hard enough for one lifetime. I have no way of knowing what my father was worth at the time they sold Schary Manor, but a good guess would be that his assets totaled over $300,000. It was a considerable fortune for two people who only thirteen years before had moved their family out of Thirteenth Avenue to the posh High Street district.

Frances had already presented Mother and Father with their first grandchild, a boy named Joel; Lil had also produced a son, Edgar. To my parents the future seemed to be a bowl of cherries. Retirement would mean the end of boarders in our home; no matter how friendly or sweet or appreciative, boarders were still boarders. It would mean the end of steaming kitchens and meal deadlines for Mother. For Father it would mean the end of countless irritations.

Lil and Frances were safely and happily married to two good men. Sam was apparently doing well in California; and while Father regretted my writing ambitions, I had proven, somewhat tentatively, that I could make a living out of my ambition by writing—and being paid for—some columns for Newark newspapers, and he was more or less resigned.

Therefore Mother and Father decided to give up the business, and were looking forward to summers on the Jersey shore (without managing hotels, which they had done) and winters in the soft air of Florida. Father began to plan a large country estate where there would be brooks, vast lawns, and houses for all the family.

It was only after their decision had been made that tragedy struck. Frances and Lou had been living with us while Lou was getting special training in a field which has since made him wealthy, when suddenly

Frances began to complain of pain and general discomfort. When she developed swollen glands in her neck, the diagnosis made in New York was that she was suffering from tubercular glands, which should be excised. As a routine measure after surgery, a biopsy was made and sent to the laboratory. Only then was it discovered that Frances was ill with Hodgkins disease, a cancer of the lymph glands. The disease was far advanced and we were told that it was incurable. The expectancy was eighteen months.

I can remember very clearly the scene when Lillian and Lou and my Father returned from New York to tell Mother. She clutched her hands and shook her head. I wish now that I had had full understanding then of what that terrible news did to her and to Father. Perhaps I could have been more comforting. But I did not truly comprehend their shock until years later when I became a parent. On the trip back to Newark, Father had resolved to go through with their retirement plans. It would give them a chance to be with Frances to help her fight the illness and possibly to prove the doctors wrong. Frances was not to be told. We braced ourselves for an ordeal. As the months passed Frances remained hopeful and in good spirits. She could walk and was driven to New York for X-ray treatments. Her decline was gradual.

When we moved out of Schary Manor, my parents took an apartment on Belmont Avenue. Lou, Frances and Joel were living with us, for Lou was often away from home because of his field work in the baking business.

On New Year's Eve, 1925, Father decided to have a celebration. It would be the first New Year's Eve in eleven years on which we had not worked, and Father decided that we must behave as if we were not carrying the sad secret that was such a burden. We went to New York for a "high time." First there was dinner at the Waldorf with wine and champagne; then we went to see *The Song of the Flame,* a new operetta. For after the theatre, Father had reserved a table at Delmonico's. This part of the evening was melancholy; while enjoying the occasion, Frances was obviously tired and not feeling well. Though we all tried to be gay, it was clear that we ought to be home, where we presently went.

It was the last time that all of us ever went out together. As winter faded into spring, Frances became bedridden. Father rented a home in Bradley Beach, and Lil and Henry came to stay for the summer. Father began a search for new doctors and new cures, and we were victimized by a variety of quacks with quick-healing devices and drugs, which drained my parents' hope and capital.

During this summer I worked again at a Y.M.H.A. camp as a dramatic counselor. When I returned to Bradley Beach after Labor Day without having seen Frances except for one weekend in July, I was more aware than anyone of the toll her illness had taken. In the fall we moved back to Newark. I was working for the *Jewish Chronicle,* Father was doing some real estate trading, Mother was involved in her charities, and Lil had her own family to take care of. But we all worried over and comforted Frances and each other as best we could. She never mentioned her illness to anyone. If she knew, as I suspect she did, she had decided that her knowledge would only be an added burden to us, and she always insisted that the next day she would feel better.

On November 5 I came home from a rehearsal of a show at the B'Nai Abraham, a program of one-act plays which I was directing. It was my first job as director, an opportunity given to me by Nathan Leibson, who had more confidence in me than I had in myself. Frances was in bed, sitting propped up on pillows. She could no longer lie back without discomfort in breathing. She and Mother had been listening over the radio to an orchestra playing "Moonlight and Roses," a song we had first heard when Sam had sung it from a radio station in California. Mother told me that for a moment Frances had cried because she thought it such a beautiful, sad song. She said to Mother, "I'd like to see Sam. I miss him."

Father was playing cards with Henry; Zaida was in his room reading; Joel was asleep; Lillian was in the kitchen making a late snack; Lou had just called from Bridgeport, where he was working, to speak to Frances. When I went in to see her we talked about her wedding five years earlier. We laughed as she recalled how upset Father had been about some relatives of his from New York, the Baggs, a family of four who Father insisted should be seated together. Each thing he had said had struck us as uproarious.

"You can't separate the Baggs."

"You have to put the Baggs all together."

"The Baggs are very close."

It wasn't funny to Pa, and the more we had giggled the more irritated he had become. It wasn't until long after the wedding that he had been able to joke about the Baggs.

Then Frances asked me to tell her how the rehearsals were going, and I gave her a full report. She had always come faithfully to see me in plays at high school and the "Y" and the temple. My first one-act play, staged at the B'Nai Abraham, was a comedy called *Out Where the West Begins,* and I was encouraged when Kenyon Nicholson read it and decided to direct it. Mother and Frances had defied a blizzard to see the performance, and Frances had told me it was to be the first of many big evenings for me. Now she wanted to know how the three one-acters were working out. As I told her about the evening I could see that she was getting tired and more uncomfortable. I suggested that she rest, but she asked me to stay and sit in her room. She would take a short nap, and afterward I could read her some poetry. She smiled, then winked at me and closed her eyes. As I watched, she leaned forward, then convulsively stiffened, and slumped back on her pillows. Before I touched her I knew that she was dead.

I called the family and then telephoned Dr. Nash. When he arrived and confirmed her death, Mother asked me to call Lou in Bridgeport. This reminded Father of an odd and painful coincidence; at Frances' birth he had had a job on the road and had received the news of her arrival in Bridgeport.

Joel woke up crying after midnight, and Father went in to comfort him. When we were little, Father often sang to us. One of his favorites was one that ran:

> All aboard for Blanket Bay
> Won't get home till the break of day.
> Bless Mommy, bless Daddy, and sail away.
> All aboard for Blanket Bay.

That night as Pa held Joel in his arms he rocked him to sleep with the same song.

23

Mammenyu, Tottenyu, Gottenyu

In the Jewish life I knew there was a trinity to whom we appealed or expressed our fears. A small accident would evoke *"Mammenyu"* (beloved Mother), a larger mishap would bring forth *"Tottenyu"* (beloved Father), and a shock would provoke *"Gottenyu"* (beloved God). A disaster could evoke an appeal to all three.

Mother, Father and God represented the core of Jewish family life. Every home depended on the warmth and care given by Mother, the strength and security given by Father, and the omnipresence and omnipotence of God. Mother was there when you were ailing or hungry or cold, Father was always handy to protect you, and God was available for everything.

While we all accepted God's will and His judgment, we did not feel it presumptuous to debate the decision with Him. (Abraham established this ancient prerogative when he bargained with God for the righteous who lived in Sodom and Gomorrah.) So when we said "*Gottenyu*," we were in effect saying, "How come this has happened?"—even though a moment before we might have been saying, "*Baruch dayan emes*" (Blessed be Thy judgment).

When Frances died I feared that our family, which was so closely knit, might become unraveled. I felt deep pain for Mother and Father and for Lou and Joel. In untimely fashion Lil, Sam and I had been deprived of a dear and beloved sister. Consequently, I questioned my faith. *Gottenyu*, I wondered, why?

But there was no answer except the one of acceptance, which we all learned from Mother. She tempered the wind and held us firm against the rains of doubt and confusion. This period of acceptance began when the *shiveh* (the mourning period) was over. Mother insisted that all of us remember that Joel, a child of four, could not be raised in an atmosphere of grief. He must hear songs and laughter; we had to play games with him and make the life around him busy and normal. As a result, our lives also became busy and normal. Since Judaism itself is a religion that talks mainly of life, we began to draw on its tenets for sustenance. Mother always said that being Jewish was a way of life, a faith of ethics; you couldn't be a good Jew by heaving a big sigh of resignation "and letting the trolley car run over you." We had to live, and in God's own time we too would have to move on and learn things we could not know or understand in this world.

So after the *shiveh* we rose from the wooden boxes
which had been our chairs for seven days and went
back to work. Soon Mother resumed her charity work at
the Home for the Aged and Father dabbled again in
real estate. Lillian and Henry had their son Edgar and
their own home to fill their time, Lou was working on
the road, and I got a new job at the Y.M.H.A. editing
a weekly newspaper.

My parents shared their loneliness and loss with
me during this time and so I came to know them better
and to love them more. From both of them I learned
the healing power of time and the sin of prolonged grief.
"Think of the good times," Mother would say. "The
good memories are always there. Remember them and
enjoy them." At first this was easier said than done, but
we tried to follow Mother's example. Gradually we began to talk about Frances and laugh at the memories
of her ineffable poise under duress; of her indifference
to housework and cooking; of her suitors who besieged
the Manor and were rejected for various reasons (one
because he had a potbelly instead of a stomach, another
because he wore green suits that made Frances nause-
ated, another who had the misfortune to lose some
bridgework while he was eating corn-on-the-cob).

Of course I had gone on with my job of directing
the three one-act plays at the Temple B'Nai Abraham.
On the night of the opening Mother insisted on being
there, and Lil came from New York to join her in watching my first directorial job. They were extravagant in
their praise and reported all to Pa, who listened skep-
tically.

As time passed I resumed my nightly prayers; I

had made my peace with God. Mother was pleased that I no longer considered myself a lost member of the tribe.

Today only my brother Sam and myself are left, but our memories are warm and rich, and we cherish and enjoy them as Mother told us to do.

Sometimes I still murmur, *"Gottenyu,"* but I also try to remember a certain night when I came home after seeing the Broadway production of Paul Green's *In Abraham's Bosom*. I told Mother how moved I had been by the play, and then we spoke of my dreams and ambitions. I said that the years ahead would be frustrating and perhaps fruitless, but that I was committed to the theatre. Mother listened, nodded her head and said, "Believe me, Sonny, with help from God your dreams can come true." Then she smiled. "But God is very busy, so don't forget to do your share of the work."

It was the wisest thing Mother ever said to me.

About the Author

Born in Newark, New Jersey, in 1905, Dore Schary early developed an interest in the theatre and in dramatic writing which found its first complete expression when he served as "dramatic counselor" at a summer camp in the Catskills. In 1932 he went to Hollywood, and for the next eight years wrote constantly for the screen. Among his many screen plays during this period was *Boys Town*, which won him an Academy Award.

From 1943 to 1956 Mr. Schary served in various executive capacities for the Selznick organization, RKO, and MGM. Since then he has devoted his time exclusively to writing and to the New York theatre. *Sunrise at Campobello*, his first play, was an instantaneous hit which won many prizes. He has also been involved, either as writer, director, or coproducer—and sometimes as all three—with *A Majority of One*, *The Highest Tree*, *The Unsinkable Molly Brown*, *The Devil's Advocate*, *Something About a Soldier* and his current play, *Banderol*.

Mr. Schary has contributed articles and stories to such publications as the New York *Times*, the *Saturday Review*, the *Atlantic* and the *Reporter*. His book, *Case History of a Movie*, published by Random House in 1950, is considered definitive on the mechanics, arithmetic and artistry of movie-making.